I Am Not Superwoman

FURTHER ESSAYS ON HAPPIER LIVING

Michele Woodward

Designed, edited, and produced by Michele Woodward Consulting, Inc.

Limits of Liability/Disclaimer of Warranty:

Both the writer and publisher have prepared this book to the best of their abilities. However, neither the writer nor the publisher makes any representation or warranties as to the accuracy, applicability, or completeness of this book. They disclaim any warranties (expressed or implied), merchantability, or appropriateness for a specific purpose. Neither the writer nor the publisher, under any circumstances, shall be held liable for any loss or other damages of any kind. As always, please seek the advice of a competent legal, tax, accounting, or other professional. Neither the writer nor the publisher warrant the performance, effectiveness or applicability of any sites listed in this book. All links are for informational purposes only and are not warranted for content, accuracy or any other implied or explicit purpose. This manual contains material protected under International and Federal Copyright Laws and Treaties. Any unauthorized reprint or use of this material is prohibited.

Copyright:
I Am Not Superwoman: Further Essays On Happier Living is Copyright © 2010, Michele Woodward .
All Rights Reserved.

ISBN: 1452856052
ISBN-13: 9781452856056

For Munroe & Grace
Reminders that every day is a gift.

Table of Contents

Introduction	vii
I Am Not Superwoman	1
Mama Ain't Happy	5
Life In The Balance	11
Always Let Them See You Sweat	17
I'm Sorry, I Can't	23
Busy But Not Productive	29
What's The Point?	35
The Power of You	41
The One	45
Your Hidden Treasure	51
Got Envy?	57
Your New Yardstick	63
Failure To Execute	67
What's Not Working?	73
The Expectations Of Others	77
A New Normal	83
Would You Like Fries With That?	87
W-O-R-K (A Four Letter Word)	93
Finding A Job 2.0	99
Smart Networking	105
Finally Un-Stuck	111
The Integrity Thing	117
Love Your Work? (What Are You, Crazy?)	123
When Your Job Is A Soul-Sucking Hellhole	129
When Gifts Become Junk	135

Make Your Own Thanksgiving	139
Money Changes Everything	145
More On Money	151
How To Tell A Story	157
3 Ways To Get Out Of Your Own Way	163
What's Your Why?	169
You.	173
More Than Anything	179
Loving Change	185
Change Or Die	191
Solving Problems	197
Pay For It	203
Do Less, Get More	209
The Simplest Solution	213
Start At The End	217
Acknowledgements	221

Introduction

I write every week. Since November, 2006, I've written one essay each week. Rain or shine. Snow or hail. Dust bunnies under the fridge or not. I am just that disciplined.

Or stupid. It could go either way, some weeks.

I publish these essays on my blog, and, over time, readers ask me to pull them together into a book. Hence, *Lose Weight, Find Love, De-Clutter & Save Money: Essays on Happier Living* (BookSurge, 2008), and now comes *I Am Not Superwoman: Further Essays on Happier Living* (CreateSpace, 2010).

In this book you'll find essays on – surprise – happier living, but you'll also learn about money and how to make it work for you. You'll learn how to change difficult relationships. You'll finally figure out how to get un-stuck and say no.

Finally.

I work hard to provide you with practical, tactical, humorous approaches to the things that vex you. Because a sense of humor is often the best tool on your belt.

These essays were written between 2008 and 2010 – and during that time, I dealt with some personal challenges, including thyroid cancer. While I can happily say, "I am disease free" today, there were some weeks when that prognosis wasn't completely certain. It's my hope that readers who are facing their own challenges will find comfort, direction and solace in these pages.

I continue to write each week. If you'd like to receive my essays in your email in-box, please go to www.lifeframeworks.com and register to get them every week.

And, thank you. Thank you for buying this book. Thank you for reading these words. Thanks for making your own steps toward a happier life. Because, together, we can create a much happier world.

Michele Woodward
May, 2010
Arlington, VA

I Am Not Superwoman

THERE APPEAR TO BE MANY WOMEN WHO HOPE TO CONVINCE themselves and the rest of us that they are perfect. Hair — perfectly coiffed, colored and curled. Body — athletic and toned. Wardrobe — trendy, sexy and stylish. Children — well-behaved high achievers. Husband — handsome, wealthy, attentive.

They think they need to be Superwoman. They want everything to be perfect.

But, honey, I know what's going on inside.

In the push to be perfect, they feel anything but. Life is a series of experiences where they are not enough, and can't possibly do enough. They look at the women around them and feel inferior, and hide that they're totally struggling to keep up. They grit their teeth and smile through the stress of Superwoman expectations.

Because I'm a life coach, people often expect me to live that perfect life. Yesterday I was in a shop that sells my book *Lose Weight, Find Love, De-Clutter & Save Money: Essays on Happier Living* and the store manager said, looking down her aquiline nose at me, "Do you live what you write?" I smiled sweetly and said, "Absolutely."

And I do. But let me share a little something that may just make tomorrow a little easier for all you would-be Superwomen:

I am not Superwoman. Not even close.

Sometimes my only wardrobe concern is: Am I clean?

My house generally, at all times, needs vacuuming.

I have been known to feed my children take-out. Frequently.

I often forget to return phone calls and am terrible at remembering birthdays.

I can overbook my calendar.

Gasp! I am divorced.

No, I'm not Superwoman. And I'm really, really glad for that. Because what I am is 100% Michele. I have four priorities and if I can handle those every day, I am doing a pretty good job. Want to know what they are? Be present with my kids and everyone else I meet. Care for my physical, financial, emotional and spiritual health. Learn. Lead.

That's it. That's *all.* Hair, nails, make-up, shoes? If I get to it, I get to it.

Yep, I am Imperfecta Girl, and I absolutely 100% love my perfectly imperfect life.

If you're struggling to get it right, to be perfect, to have it all, let me ask you: Can you get to the place where you give up attempting to be a mythical Superwoman, and find the place where you're a true Imperfecta Girl — authentically yourself, happy with exactly what you have, comfortable in your own skin, serving your own priorities? Go on, give it a try. All you have to lose is stress. All you have to gain is your true self. And it will be absolutely OK with me if you don't do it perfectly.

Mama Ain't Happy

There appear to be many women who hope to convince themselves and the rest of us that they are perfect. Hair — perfectly coiffed, colored and curled. Body — athletic and toned. Wardrobe — trendy, sexy and stylish. Children — well-behaved high achievers. Husband — handsome, wealthy, attentive.

They think they need to be Superwoman. They want everything to be perfect.

But, honey, I know what's going on inside.

In the push to be perfect, they feel anything but. Life is a series of experiences where they are not enough, and can't possibly do enough. They look at the women around them and feel inferior, and hide that they're totally struggling to keep up. They grit their teeth and smile through the stress of Superwoman expectations.

Because I'm a life coach, people often expect me to live that perfect life. Yesterday I was in a shop that sells my book *Lose Weight, Find Love, De-Clutter & Save Money: Essays on Happier Living* and the store manager said, looking down her aquiline nose at me, "Do you live what you write?" I smiled sweetly and said, "Absolutely."

And I do. But let me share a little something that may just make tomorrow a little easier for all you would-be Superwomen:

I am not Superwoman. Not even close.

Sometimes my only wardrobe concern is: Am I clean?

My house generally, at all times, needs vacuuming.

I have been known to feed my children take-out. Frequently.

I often forget to return phone calls and am terrible at remembering birthdays.

I can overbook my calendar.

Gasp! I am divorced.

No, I'm not Superwoman. And I'm really, really glad for that. Because what I am is 100% Michele. I have four priorities and if I can handle those every day, I am doing a pretty good job. Want to know what they are? Be present with my kids and everyone else I meet. Care for my physical, financial, emotional and spiritual health. Learn. Lead.

That's it. That's *all.* Hair, nails, make-up, shoes? If I get to it, I get to it.

Yep, I am Imperfecta Girl, and I absolutely 100% love my perfectly imperfect life.

If you're struggling to get it right, to be perfect, to have it all, let me ask you: Can you get to the place where you give up attempting to be a mythical Superwoman, and find the place where you're a true Imperfecta Girl — authentically yourself, happy with exactly what you have, comfortable in your own skin, serving your own priorities? Go on, give it a try. All you have to lose is stress. All you have to gain is your true self. And it will be absolutely OK with me if you don't do it perfectly.

Turns out women aren't happy.

Turns out the older women get, the sadder they become.

Turns out once she hits 47 years old, a woman's happiness declines quite steadily.

Or so I read an article in the Huffington Post, written by Marcus Buckingham.

Buckingham is a smart guy — his work has transformed the way we talk about work and life by shifting our collective focus from shoring up weaknesses to centering in strengths.

I like him.

So back to this women-are-increasingly-unhappy idea… what's the deal?

In the article, Buckingham says it's not because women are paid less than men, although that is a fact. Nor is it because women assume more of the household chores than their male partners. Also a fact. And it's not because women have limited opportunities. Because we have so many more opportunities than our grandmothers did.

Why are women aging unhappily?

Of course, I have a theory.

Let's call it the Disillusionment Theory.

From the work I do with women, it seems that for a certain generation the message we got growing up was, "Be a good girl, don't have strong opinions or talk too much, get along, be pretty enough to catch a husband, have kids and then everything will be easy for you."

And what happens to many women by the time they turn 47? The kids you put your life on hold for are grown up and have their own lives. The husband you put through medical school left the marriage. The parents who defined you as their darling good girl have died. Your body's not the same. The media tells you that you're no longer pretty enough or young enough to catch a man's eye, let alone a second husband. It's grim.

Because your whole life you played by the rules, but in mid-life the rules seem to have changed. Life is not easy.

Nothing's the way it should be.

But we know, and Buckingham documents, there are women who find deep happiness and satisfaction despite the loss trajectory of their lives. What do they have that other women don't?

Buckingham gives us some juicy tidbits about the happiest women — they:

- Don't agonize over who they aren't—they accept and act on who they are. They have discovered the role they were born to play and they play it.
- Don't juggle—they catch-and-cradle. They don't keep things at bay, but select a few things and draw them in close.
- Don't strive for balance—they strive for fullness. They intentionally imbalance their lives toward those moments that make them feel strong.
- Always sweat the small stuff—They know and act on the specific details of what invigorates them (and they let go of what doesn't strengthen them).

So, to be happy at mid-life, women have to focus on what makes them happy and do more of that. And they have to let go of what no longer makes them happy. They need to find new ways to define themselves — based on their strengths — and drop the old ways they were defined.

In terms I use as a coach, to be happy in mid-life women need to move from living in their "social selves", concerned with What Other People Will Think, to living firmly in their "authentic selves", which is who they are at their very core.

Calls to mind Laurel Thatcher Ulrich's famous quip, "Well-behaved women seldom make history." Perhaps especially in mid-life, it's "Well-behaved women are seldom happy."

Y'know what? I choose happy. If that makes me appear less well-behaved, then so be it. And you are welcome to join me.

And for my fabulous guy readers – if there is a woman in your life who is approaching the happiness tipping point, what can you do? Try this: encourage her to misbehave. Encourage her to step out and step up. Throw away the old rules, and join her in making some new ones. Believe me – you will love it. By encouraging the woman you love to be more fully herself, you will be amazed at the joy and happiness that will flood your life. She'll be more her, which only allows you… to be more you.

Life In The Balance

"Suffering is normal."

"Work is supposed to be hard."

"I have to keep busy."

"No pain, no gain."

"Idle hands are the Devil's playground."

"Life is not supposed to be easy."

Damn that Protestant Work Ethic.

It's those deeply ingrained PWE messages that hold us back from making changes leading to more satisfaction, happiness and meaning. We're all so nose-to-the-grindstone, unhappy-as-hell, but-hey-what-can-I-do-about-it people.

What frustrated folks may not know is this: the key to a balanced life is a fair measure of joy. Of purposeless fun. Of play.

Which is diametrically opposed the good old PWE.

Know what I mean? We take something that is supposed to be joyful fun, like, oh... running through a forest, feeling the wind on your skin and your hair, smelling the fragrance of the deep woods, spying a shy fawn, or a curious fox. And we turn it into, "Gotta go nine today so I'll be ready for the marathon."

Sure, having a purpose gives us something to strive for, but often bypasses the underlying joy of simply doing a thing we love.

A woman I know was lamenting this week that her just conferred Master's degree didn't seem to be that valuable in this job market. I asked, "Why did you decide on that field of study?" She answered, "Because I was really interested in it, and I thought it would be fun." I paused a moment. "So you enjoyed the learning?" She said, "Oh, yes!" I asked, "Isn't that enough?"

Learning for learning's sake – ever known that feeling?

To achieve balance in your life, sometimes you need to allow yourself to do something for the sheer fun of it – and not because it will lead to something else. Something "productive." If you have the time, the money and the interest, why not take a class? Or get a Master's degree? Or a PhD, for that matter? With no eye toward where it will "get" you?

Why not enjoy yourself?

There's a point that comes in everyone's life – and for some of us it comes more than once – when you know things have to change. Yet you ignore the stirrings of your heart, the urgings of your soul, because making a change might seem indulgent.

Which is a definite PWE no-no.

There's the doctor who would really like to open a bead shop, but how would that look? All those years of medical school – a waste?

Or the lawyer who would like to be a non-profit case worker. Law school down the drain?

Or the one-time-CPA mom who would like to go back to work, but do something that doesn't involve numbers. At all. Ever. Shouldn't she just keep up her certification, just in case?

Not necessarily.

We are all the sum total of our life's experiences. I know that nothing I've ever done in my life – the good, the bad, the extremely ugly – was a waste. It's all added up to make me the person I am today, and that feels pretty daggone good.

When you get the chance to reinvent your life, you get the chance to use everything you've got. When you get the chance to increase your joy, and, nifty by-product, achieve that elusive life balance, take it. Regardless of the little messages that tell you that following your heart is indulgent or purposeless.

If you are stuck, or itchy, or worried, or out of balance – forget the PWE. Focus on joy. And the rest will follow.

༄

Always Let Them See You Sweat

So, here's the thing.

In an effort to appear calm and confident…

In an attempt to be kinda cool…

In adopting the detached pose of the uber-jaded…

Some have decided that the only way to succeed at work is to never let anyone see you sweat. As if the tag line to an '80s commercial was the Golden Rule.

And I can understand where this comes from. Really. Chickens with their heads cut off rarely engender confidence.

But.

If what you're doing looks effortless and – poof! – produced just as easy as that… when, in point of fact, you have been working 16 hours a day for 10 days with 75 people on your team in order to produce that singular, flawless product… there's a disconnect there.

And bystanders and bosses might think, "Hey, what she's doing is not that hard. Any idiot can do it."

And you don't get the raise.

Or the bonus.

Or the contract.

And I know this how? Because it's happened to me. Fairly recently.

I was asked to provide a proposal for something I do very well. I created a crackerjack plan, and priced it accordingly. And was told, "It's not that much work. We'll pay you half."

Honey, it was every bit as much work as I proposed. Maybe even more. But, see – when I have done this work in the past, I have made it look easy. Too easy. So people think it's no big thing. And not worth paying for, because it's…no big thing.

{In case you're wondering, I turned down the opportunity to work for half-price, thank you very much.}

When I coach clients who are starting their own businesses – especially coaches and consultants – self-underpricing, self-undervaluing is a real Achilles heel. Especially for women. We want to look cool, calm and collected. We want to look professional. Maybe we hold a position no woman has ever held before. Or we feel weird about money.

So we say, "Sure, I can produce that for you," even though we know it will take a miracle, two fortuitous accidents and some pixie dust to pull it off. And with any luck (we cross our fingers) we'll break even.

But, never, under any circumstances, will we let the client know how hard it was to do.

Which means they may not pay the value of the solution you offer. Or balk at your bill when you send it.

Or let you go when the budget needs some trimming.

Don't be a quiet sufferer. Instead, be the kind of person who says, "What you're asking is hard, but I think I can do it." Be the kind of person who is truly authentic about how much work is involved. Be the person who says, right up front, "What you're asking will take me 40 hours to do at $X/hour. I'll need two other people. And I can get it to you by Tuesday the 10th. How's that going to work for you?"

And after you've delivered, rather than the rote saying of, "No big deal", feel free to say, "It was a lot of work, but I'm really happy with the way it turned out."

Value what you do, my friends, and others will, too.

Word to the wise – make sure you use the "I" pronoun. Ever noticed that when talking about work success men almost always say "I" while women often default to "we"? Women tend to be collegial and consensus-building kinds of leaders and managers, and have a difficult time taking individual credit. Think about it, though: which pronoun properly places credit where credit is due?

"I", of course.

So, say "I", and if you want to recognize members of your team who did a good job – because you're fabulous you will want to – go ahead and say, "Tom really managed the spreadsheets" or "Megan was super with the contractors" or "Denise kept all the trains running on time." Your people will appreciate the individual shout-out, and credit will be properly spread around.

Let me bottom-line this for you: when you let people see exactly how much effort you're putting in — when you let them see an appropriate amount of sweat — you are giving them a way to understand the value of what you produce. Each drop of sweat adds to your perceived value. Each drop of sweat seals your expertise and ability.

So, forget deodorant commercials and their irksome jingles. Do yourself a favor: *Always* let them see you sweat.

You're a superstar. All you've got to do is…let it show.

I'm Sorry,
I Can't

Let me tell you about Meg. She's smart, she's kind, she's hard-working. She's always willing to pitch in and help out.

She's great.

She's also extremely stressed, crazy busy and frazzled. There are never enough hours in the day. She can't do anything fully, or calmly, or right. She's past maximum capacity, verging on overload. Every. Single. Minute. Of. Every. Single. Day.

Her biggest problem? Is it her job, her kids, her husband, her aging mom?

Guess again.

Somewhere along the line, she either never realized she could, or completely forgot that she was able to, set her own priorities.

Somewhere along the line, she let other people's priorities determine where she put her time and attention.

And as a result, she is stressed, crazy busy and frazzled.

And she doesn't think she really knows who she is anymore. Because while she can tell you what's important to nearly anyone else, she can't really tell you what's important to herself.

Women, particularly, are socialized from the cradle to say, "Yes." As in, "Yes, I will stir the sauce. Yes, I will set the table. Yes, I will patch that hole. Yes, I will eat at your favorite restaurant. Yes, I will take the last, misshapen, half-iced cupcake - that is, unless you want it."

Women can feel uncomfortable and icky, then, when they find themselves in a situation where they might, possibly, have to say something sorta kinda possibly close to the n-word - you know the word I mean: "No."

Our biggest worry is that if we say "No", then someone won't like us.

And if we're not liked, we're not OK.

OK is what is stamped on papers when approval is given. So we fear that if we say "No", we won't get the stamp of approval.

But - you know me - I have to ask: the approval of whom?

People who want you to attend to their priorities first, now, immediately? {insert foot-stomping here}

We call those demanding, foot-stomping people "bullies", by the way.

When we say "Yes" when we mean "No", we put our own needs, priorities, dreams and desires on the back burner. We neglect our own sovereignty, to use a term my friend, the writer Hiro Boga writes about very eloquently.

When we lose our sovereignty, we lose our personhood and become an extension of someone else. And a servant of their needs, priorities, dreams and desires.

We get lost.

So what do you do? How do you make the change, after a lifetime of "Yes"? How do you acknowledge that saying "No" is really hard? And more than a bit scary?

You say, "I'm sorry, I can't." You say, "I'm sorry" because probably you really are. Probably you worry about approval, and acceptance, and you're sorry that you're disappointing the person you've always said "Yes" to. So, go ahead, say "I'm sorry" because that's what you feel.

And over time, you'll find that you need to apologize less and less. You'll find, too, that the primary person whose approval you seek, is... you.

You'll find that by saying "I'm sorry, I can't" to energy-sucking, person-losing stuff, you open up wide spaces to be able to say, with conviction, "You bet I can" to the things that really matter to you.

༄

Busy But Not Productive

ONE THING THAT ABSOLUTELY DRIVES ME NUTTY is busyness. Busy, busy, busy - say it fast enough and you buzz like a bee. Which is, apparently, quite a good thing, as we often say, "Busy as a bee."

And maybe we get a buzz from all that busyness. When we're busy, we belong to the collective hive of others who are busy, too. Buzz, buzz, buzz, we're all in motion together.

Let me ask you this: are you busy for the sake of being busy, or are you actually doing something?

What do you have to show for all of your flitting around? Anything?

At all?

First bees and now athletes - I'm going metaphor-crazy. But hang with me, will you?

When I watch the Olympics every couple of years, I'm struck by the efficiency of the athletes. I have watched skiers, eyes closed, visualizing the run they are about to take. Virtually practicing, they move their bodies as if they are edging through the gates at ninety miles an hour.

And I've watched figure skaters who put their hand here, their hip there, their toe spike down precisely at this point in a jump. That's the only way they can land the quadruple toe loop.

But probably the most efficient athletes I've watched have been the ski jumpers. They launch, they move right into position, they fly.

All of these athletes practice, practice, practice until their discrete moves become muscle memory and more than second nature.

Know what else they have? They have a goal in mind - to win, sure. But also to be better than the last time they skated, skied or jumped. To have a better score, or to shave off two tenths of a second. That's a win.

So for you to turn your busyness into productivity, you, too, must have a goal in mind and move efficiently toward it.

Which also means you have to have priorities. Because you can have four million goals to reach, but if none are sorted by importance you'll spend ten seconds on each and accomplish nothing.

Which is not the way Olympic athletes train. They spend hours on one arm position. On where their knees should be on landing. On positioning their poles.

Take a piece of paper and write down all the things you do in a day. [Competitive? Then write down everything you do in a week.] Group them into broad categories, like Work, Kids, Spouse, Home, Bill Paying, Mom, Exercise, Professional Whittling (hey, it's OK to have a hobby). Then look at your categories. Does work support your kids, or do kids support your work? Compare each category this way and you will ultimately have a sorted list of your priorities.

Voila.

There's another step.

Look at your list of priorities. Which lights you up and brings joy to your life? If that thing or things are low down on your list, then perhaps the reason you're not productive is the conflict between what your heart wants and what your mind wants. Spend some time sorting out this piece and you'll find that perhaps you can care less about your work identity - which will free up time and space to serve your parenting priority. Or your inner whittler.

Once you have your priorities in alignment, see which you need to attend to now, which can wait, and which can be dropped. If you are still tying your sixteen year old's sneakers, trust me, you can let that go. Obsessively worrying about next Christmas can wait. Fixing the hole in the roof? That's a now thing.

There is no point in being busy for the sake of being busy. It's all wasted movement that generates nothing.

"Life's but a walking shadow, a poor player

That struts and frets his hour upon the stage

And then is heard no more: it is a tale

Told by an idiot, full of sound and fury,

Signifying nothing." (The Tragedy of Macbeth, Act 5, Scene 5, by William Shakespeare)

Signify something. Drop the busyness in favor of efficient productivity. And the only buzz in your life will come from seeing all that you've accomplished.

What's The Point?

THIS ONE IS COMING FROM THE HEART.

One week, after a particularly challenging coaching session with a client, I wrote this on my Facebook page:

"Never confuse urgency and drama with meaning and purpose."

So many people are focused on "winning" and "making a mark" and "getting" and being "Type A" and, then ask me to help them find out why they are so unhappy and unfulfilled and struggle to identify their life's purpose.

I can tell you something. They're making things a lot more difficult than they need to be.

Because I believe every human being has the exact same purpose in life.

It's to be a force for good in the world.

Simple.

And although we share the same *purpose*, we derive our own personal *meaning* from how we decide to do good.

One person might be a force for good in the world by teaching. Another by cleaning streets. One might find meaning in helping people become prosperous, another in curing illness.

The overarching purpose is to do something good. In large and small ways. All the time.

I am never doing good if I cheat you, scam you or otherwise take advantage of you. Never. Not in business.

Not ever. People who conduct their business this way may find that they get a big score at the outset, but rarely ever create a lasting, truly lucrative business. See Bernie Madoff, for example. You do better when you're focused on doing good.

Now, tyrants and despots often justify their bad acts by saying they are acting in the "common good." Ethnic cleansing, silencing dissidents and controlling the media comes to mind. You can probably come up with some other examples yourself.

But when anyone is hurt, good is not being done. When harm is done, we're acting in direct opposition to our life's purpose, so it's no wonder that tyrants and despots often wind up being hung by their ankles with body parts stuffed into their mouths by the very people they were trying to "protect."

Now we know what meaning and purpose are all about — let's look at urgency and drama.

Just because something's urgent, doesn't mean it's important. If I get a flat tire, it's urgent but it's not really important. I can pull over, jack up the car, replace the tire, go on my way.

Or I can choose to make it a drama. Boy howdy, can I. How about I call my brother, my sister-in-law, my neighbor, my son, my best friend and the local radio station to announce that I Have A Flat Tire and invite them to join the pity party with me? I can then regale the folks at the supermarket, the dry cleaners and the smoothie shop with the story of My Flat Tire. Watch me work the story at the office!

I get all wrapped around the axle.

And a twenty minute inconsequential period extends into hours, maybe even weeks of drama.

Which takes time and attention away from my real life's purpose.

Cuz I'm not doing good. In fact, I'm just creating needless motion that uses up my energy.

Which is what I hear from my coaching clients. For years and years they have allowed urgent matters to masquerade as their life's purpose, and accepted drama as a substitute for meaning. They're addicted to the high fructose corn syrup adrenaline rush of drama, and have completely lost their taste for the true sweetness of real meaning.

When you're hip to your life's purpose of being a force for good, you can find meaning in the smallest things. Like holding the door open for the pregnant woman pushing a stroller. Like giving up your seat on the subway to the elderly man with the cane. Like smiling. Easy things you can do every day.

Big things can hold great meaning, too. Like mentoring that young man at work. Or being generous with well-deserved raises to your best people despite the economy. Or finding a vaccine for cancer. Challenging, time consuming things that can take a whole career to accomplish are ripe with meaning.

Since this is my own personal manifesto, let me go a step further. I believe you already know this. I believe people are, at their core, good. We only get stuck when we get in our own way and confuse urgency and drama with meaning and purpose. So step out of the way. Deal with that which is urgent, because we all face things that need attention. But attend without drama. Fulfilling your life purpose means being who it is you are at your core — good old you — and doing what good you can in each moment.

∽

The Power Of You

THERE'S A QUOTE I PARTICULARLY LOVE... DO YOU know it?

"Our deepest fear is not that we are inadequate. Our deepest fear is that we are powerful beyond measure."

(Marianne Williamson, *A Return to Love,* Harper, 1996)

When I work with people — whether they're looking for a job, or trying to do the job they have better, whether they have a big decision to make or a crisis to handle — they focus on where they feel weak. Time after time I see people stuck and wallowing in their deficit, when the only solution is to stand in their strengths.

To allow themselves to be powerful beyond measure.

What do I mean? How do you shift from a position of weakness to strength?

It's not waiting for someone else to give you permission to do what's best for you.

It's saying what you need to say — including the word "no" — rather than what you're expected to say.

It's doing more of what you're good at and that you like, rather than doing things that sap you.

It's about knowing, deeply, yourself and loving everything about you. Even the extra pounds, the bad hair days, the annoying habits, the fear. 'Cuz once you love that about yourself, you are open to loving it about others.

When you stand in your power, you become powerful beyond measure. I'm not talking about the kind of power that gives you dominion over others or makes you rich or famous. I'm talking about the kind of power that makes you clear. Happy. Certain. Authentic.

I'm talking about the power that you already have inside you. I'm talking about The Power of You.

It's right there inside you — all your strengths, gifts and talents. All you have to do is use them. Every day. And you will profoundly change your life.

∾

The One

She asked me, "Do you think he could be The One?"

I looked at her hopeful face and wondered how she would take my heartfelt answer — no, honey, he's not The One. He might be a wonderful guy, and you might be extremely happy with him, but he's not The One.

Because there's no such thing as The One.

Despite everything you've been told, The One is a myth that only serves to hold us back and make us wretchedly unhappy.

Because there's not just one person in the whole world who you can love — there are millions.

Pick your jaw up from the floor, sweetie, and bear with me here.

When you decide that there's only one person out there with whom you can be happy, be contented, be yourself, be deeply committed with — well, you're setting a limit. A big limiting limit.

Still don't believe me? Ok, when you say that there's only one person you can love, what about the woman I knew who was widowed when her young husband was killed in his tank in the Battle of the Bulge? To say that he was The One — the only person she could possibly ever love — what does that say about her second marriage which thrived for fifty years? The one in which she was happy, contented, herself, and deeply committed? Was it wrong? Which marriage didn't count?

Is it possible that both husbands could have been The One?

Starting to understand? OK, let's talk about this in the simple terms of abundance and lack. Abundance means having lots and lack means having very little, or, worse, none at all. Believing in The One sets up a deep, black, lack hole. Coming from a lack mindset, I think that I may only get one shot at happiness, so I better get it right. I better be picky. Or, I better hold on to a mediocre boyfriend because what if he's The One? What if this is as good as it gets?

Abundance is just the opposite. Abundance means that there are many people I can love and be committed to. So if you hit me, or steal my money, or treat me like dirt — I'm a-walking. Because I know, deep down, that there is someone else out there I can love. Plenty of someone elses.

Now, I have to say this: I am a friend of marriage in general, and a friend of your marriage in particular. I am not saying that living in abundance allows you to have affairs all willy-nilly and be off the hook because you're just living in abundance, dude, and all your partners are The Ones. Huh-uh.

Knowing that there are many people you can love yet acknowledging that you have chosen your spouse is how you divorce-proof your marriage.

Borrowing what I know from weight loss coaching, putting anything off limits creates a lack and only serves to place that "bad food" right smack dab at the top of your mind, increasing your desire to have that "bad food". To foil that impulse, it's important to tell yourself that you can have **any** food — but you're choosing that which is healthy.

Imagine how different you might take an office crush with this mindset. Rather than wondering, "Maybe my spouse isn't really The One. Maybe the office crush is The One. If he wasn't The One would I be feeling all these feelings?"

Naturally, you'd be feeling the crush! Because he's one of The Ones you could possibly love. But he's just **one** of The Ones. Knowing that there is plenty of love available to you puts the crush into perspective and allows you to stay committed to the person you're committed to.

And I have noticed that people carry over The One idea to their careers. Some people have an attitude that their job should be The One. Which is, again, coming from a lack place. People stay too long in jobs when they worry that maybe this is as good as it gets. Maybe working somewhere else would be harder. Or worse. Or just have different jerks.

My first job out of college was great — I worked with a terrific team of peers, and I'm happily connected with them today. It was a challenging and affirming job. But had I stayed there, I would never have had the tremendous experience of working at The White House. Which was, in a word, amazing. And had I not left The White House (well, the Secret Service would have escorted me out one way or the other after the new President took office), I would never have worked for Anne Wexler and have had five inspiring and educational years with her.

And, of course, I would not be the coach I am today without all those experiences.

I loved them all. They were each The One. And The Ones keep on coming. Because I live in abundance and happily welcome them with open arms.

Oh, there are many ways to be happy, darlings. When you know that there's is plenty to choose from — not just One, but Many — you can live in non-desperate abundance and make sound, fulfilling choices. And you'll find yourself surrounded in love. With all The Ones that are out there for you.

∽

Your Hidden Treasure

Once upon a time a baby girl was born to loving parents. On the day of her birth they gave her a beautiful box, a treasured gift. By her second birthday, the loving parents had died and the little girl was living with her aunt.

Now, Auntie was a mean-spirited, angry and bitter old woman. As the girl grew into a lovely young woman, Auntie would remind her, "You're no better than anyone else", and "Don't get too big for your britches", and, more painfully, "You are as ugly as your mother", for Auntie had doted on the girl's father and ignorantly blamed the girl's mother for his death.

So, the girl grew up believing that she was, indeed, unattractive, and hid herself behind unfashionable and unflattering clothes.

At school, the girl worked hard and excelled at her studies. In fifth grade, jealous and deceitful Teacher took her aside and said, "You're not as smart as you think you are — you're just lucky. Once your luck fades, you will fail." The girl did not know that luck was more important than hard work. Auntie had never told her that. She began to worry more about her luck running out than her studies, and soon her grades began to fall. "Teacher was right," she thought. "I am not smart. Auntie is right, too. Who do I think I am, anyway?"

The girl struggled to finish her schooling and began to look for a job. Auntie said, "Don't aim too high, you'll be disappointed," so the girl took a job cleaning offices. It was difficult, dirty, boring work, but the girl believed she was not smart enough to do anything else. Hadn't Teacher said? Hadn't Auntie said?

Every day she rode the bus to work. One day Nice Man started a conversation with the girl. She liked how his eyes twinkled. He had a kind face. He was a happy fellow. He asked her to go with him for a cup of coffee. Now, the girl had never been on a date with a boy before because Auntie had told her that all men, save her dead father, were useless bullies. "Men are interested in only one thing," Auntie would say. "And once they get it, they dump you in a hot second." The girl did not know what to do — this man seemed nice. But he might be fooling her.

She did not trust her own instincts. Auntie had been right about so many things - perhaps she was right about men and relationships. So with a sad shake of the head she said no to the coffee, and from that day on did not talk to any men.

Ten years later the girl was numb, living the same kind of small, safe life Auntie led. She was old before her time. That spring, Auntie died. The girl did not know what to do. She had looked to Auntie for so much. How could she - an old, ugly, stupid cleaning lady - make it in the world, all alone?

As she cleaned the small house she shared with Auntie, she found the beautiful box her parents had given her on the day of her birth. She did not know what it was as spiteful Auntie had hidden the treasure away. The girl gently lifted the lid and a small piece of paper fluttered to her feet.

She opened it. It was from her parents. It said, "You are the treasure. May you live a life worthy of all of your gifts."

Your Hidden Treasure 55

Inside the box was an intricately engraved silver mirror. The girl took the beautiful, cool metal in her hands and held it up to her face.

With a blinding flash, the girl saw what her parents had seen in her even as a baby. She saw clearly into her own heart and she was astonished. Rather than the ugly woman she had thought herself for so many years, suddenly she saw a lovely young woman. Was that her? Was she really that pretty?

In a moment, her limiting thoughts about herself fell away. She was beautiful, for she could see that clearly with her parents' gift. She was able to love, for she had loved even unlovable Auntie. And she was smart, because she had figured out these things about herself.

And she knew, too, that all of those things had been inside her, hidden her whole life, because that's how others had wanted it to be. She had been made to act small so that others could feel big. She straightened her spine at that thought, and vowed to never again allow herself to be framed by what others thought about her.

The next day the girl sold Auntie's house, quit her job, enrolled in college and began her life anew, knowing that her greatest treasure was within her. It always had been there, and always would be.

Moral of the story: To live fully, you must live without limits — whether imposed by yourself or imposed by others. Everything you need to be your best self is already within you. That is your greatest treasure.

Got Envy?

I'M JUST GOING TO SAY IT.

Some of us are frozen in time and space because of jealousy.

Some of us are so gripped with envy that we grasp and sabotage and act in ways unprincipled, just to get what we "want."

The ick fairly drips when it comes to jealousy and envy.

Yet, it's totally human and I'll bet you that we've each run up against jealousy, the fear that you're going to be betrayed and lose something important at the hands of someone else, and envy, which is the feeling of longing for something that someone else has.

We use these words interchangeably but they are quite different.

But here's the good news - both can teach you tons about what needs changing in your own life.

Let's look at envy. Suzanne (of course, it's not her real name), came to me for some coaching to improve her relationship with her boss. As she gave me the overview of her situation, she mentioned her Mortal Enemy At Work, Cathy. Cathy was a brown-nosing, idiotic, unpolished jerk who totally rubbed Suzanne the wrong way. Now, I know a coaching moment when I hear one, so I asked Suzanne to do this exercise:

> **The Envy Map**
> On a piece of paper, write down everything that ticks you off about the biggest jerk in your life. Don't edit or soften your feelings - put it all down. Be thorough. Be ruthless. Put it all out there.

Suzanne did the exercise (maybe you can do it, too, because there just might be a Mortal Enemy lurking in your life). Then, I had her read me every single item she wrote about co-worker Cathy. And a thread began to emerge - see, Cathy was the opposite of Suzanne in so many ways, and **that is precisely what pissed Suzanne off**. Where Suzanne was meticulous about her clothes and hair to the point of being a real Felix Unger, Cathy was more of a sloppy Oscar Madison. Where Suzanne respected hierarchy and rules, Cathy was a charming extrovert who got what she wanted regardless of the rules.

Suzanne told me a story - and her rage was palpable as she spit out the details - "We were walking down the hall and here comes the boss, Tom. I said, 'Hello, Tom' being respectful, and Cathy goes, 'Hey, Tom! How's it going? Want to grab a sandwich at lunch?' and I was like, I cannot believe she just did that!" I asked what the problem was. Suzanne, incredulously, said, "She asked the boss to lunch!"

I believe my response was a brilliant and insightful, "So?"

The real problem, of course, is that Cathy did easily that which Suzanne had put out-of-bounds. Suzanne wasn't really mad at Cathy - *Suzanne was mad at Suzanne* for being so rigid and formal that she was not able to craft a relationship with Tom.

This kind of understanding is what The Envy Map can do for any of us. When we take a hard look at the most difficult people in our lives and the things they do that tick us off the most, we get insight into some lost and orphaned feeling or experience we need to tend to.

Cathy was great for Suzanne, because she taught her how to create a better relationship with Tom. Suzanne began taking small steps, built a stronger alliance with her boss, and - guess what? - actually became friends with Cathy. Suzanne's work stress level went way down, and she felt happier and happier. Ultimately, she was promoted, but mostly, she feels good about herself.

Envy is always an early warning signal. When you have that encompassing feeling that someone's got something you want, the trick is to step back from plotting how to take it away from them (yes, I know what you've been planning) and step toward understanding what it is you've neglected and need to get into your life.

Your New Yardstick

I HAVE STARTED AND STOPPED THIS ESSAY SEVEN TIMES.

I have typed, back-spaced, deleted and select-all'ed myself into a frenzy.

Because I know what I want to say, but can't seem to find the way to say it in 600 words.

Maybe it needs fewer words, less typing, less snarky pun-filled humor.

Let's try simple, shall we?

Ahem.

To be happier, make your own yardstick to measure success.

Not your mom's measuring stick, not your dad's, not your suck-uppy cousin Kevin's, not your office mate's, not your boss', not your neighbor's, not TV, not Twitter, not Maxim magazine.

Don't let anyone tell you that you're a slacker if you don't work fourteen hour days, or that you're nobody if you don't travel for work. Don't listen to anyone tell you that all the cool kids are litigators. Or brand managers. Or social media gurus. Ignore those who hold that you're a loser if you're not pulling down six figures. Or seven. Plug up your ears when you hear that you are throwing away your degree and experience when you decide to start your own business. Or when you take a break from working to care for your small children, your sick father or your ill spouse.

All of that is someone else's measure of what's right for you.

What's right for you?

You decide.

Because when you gauge your life by someone else's measure, you will always come up short.

Build your yardstick with a mark for playing to your unique strengths. Scratch another line for your values, one for your passions, another for the realities of your life, and what it is that you really want.

Mark your integrity, your goals, your purpose in life.

Then stand back and take a look at what you've created.

Looks like success, doesn't it?

Failure to Execute

You don't know what to do.

Oh, you've got plenty of ideas about what you *could* do. About what's possible. About your dreams.

Or maybe you're really, really busy - pursuing a hundred leads at once and reeling from all the potential paths available to you.

But somehow nothing's really happening. Nothing's clicking.

And you're either starting to panic, or, conversely, starting to think that being where you are isn't really so bad. You can hang in there until things start to change. Whenever that might be. Someday.

Who finds this familiar? And just a teensy bit scary?

So, let's talk about it. Let's figure out why you consistently step away from making your ideas into something real, shall we?

You're falling in love with potential

It's easy to be drunk with love about what's possible. "I take this job, and I can make a million dollars and become CEO one day." Or, "If I become a joint venture partner with this famous person, my life will be easy and I'll become famous, too." And, "It's not really that bad - I bet I can make it better." And we are so in love with this vision that we fail to see that the CEO is only 32 years old and not going anywhere any time soon, or that the famous person has staff that deal with "joint venture partners" (and there are hundreds of joint venture partners), or that the thing is not bad - it's horrific - and is so toxic that hazmat is required.

The best dating advice I ever received was, "Never fall in love with potential". Had I ever followed it, I would have been saved plenty of heartache. But, after being bashed about the head and shoulders several times, I finally learned the lesson.

Today, when offered a possibility, I put potential aside and look at what's at hand with a clear eye. Does it fit with my strengths? My values? My goals? Notice I'm not asking, "Could it possibly, with a lot of work, pixie dust and spit, maybe fit?" It either fits or it doesn't. And if it fits, that's when I look at potential. Does this opportunity allow for growth? Is it fun? Is it worth my time?

You love the dream too much

Isn't it nice to have a dream? Feels so dreamy, and love-ly. We can visit our dreamy dream whenever we want, like some personalized amusement park, and lose ourselves in all the possibility. And we love the idea of the dream, and fondle the dream, and protect it. But we never make one step toward realizing the dream in our lives. The singer never takes voice lessons, the writer never types, the entrepreneur never starts a business.

Why?

Because the dream is perfect, and real life is seldom so.

If you're a dream-fondler but rather restless, here's an exercise: write down a full description of your dream. All of it. Even the minutiae. Then go back through and pick two things - just two teensy things - you can easily do to move ever-so-slightly toward making the dream real. See how that feels, try a couple more, and if you hit resistance, it may be because:

You're afraid that execution means change

Let's say your dream is to be a writer, and the teensy thing you choose is to start writing. And maybe you even begin to call yourself a writer. That might feel like a change. A redefinition. A big switch. People might laugh. You might not fit in with your friends - they don't even read books - or your family - who values brawn over brain.

Or maybe you grew up in a family that prides itself on academic and intellectual pursuits. You go to a competitive high school, and all your friends are shooting for the Ivy League. You go to a top school, and a prestigious graduate program. All is as it should be. But you're not happy. All you ever do is dream of starting your own landscaping business.

But if you become a landscaper, what will people think? What will you have in common with your Ivy League friends? With your siblings? With your parents?

The fear of loss keeps you in a job you don't like, being measured by a yardstick that's not even relevant to your dream. If you have a strong pull toward belonging and connection, you might hold on to the group's yardstick because making your own is so scary. And the group might say it's wrong.

Understandable. Hard to shake.

But so worth it when you do. Remember: the people who love you will love you whether you're a physicist or a landscaper. Whether you're a Regional Sales Manager or a writer. More importantly, *you* will like *you* when you're living your dream.

The failure to execute is the Big Kahuna of stuck. Making your dreams come alive, though, is the Big Enchilada of happiness. Go ahead. Start now.

༄

What's Not Working?

Boy, we human beings are creatures of habit. We love routines! So comfortable, isn't it, to mindlessly know what to do first, then go on to that, then move on to the next thing. Oh, we love it! The sameness of routine is so comforting.

Even if the routine sucks.

And is boring.

And might even be bad for us.

Kinda like having a habit we just can't give up.

But it's known and comfortable and predictable.

Which makes us feel safe.

And sometimes feel stuck.

It's at this moment of awareness of our stuckness that we need to stop, and think, and ask, "What's not working?" It's a scary question, most certainly, but an eminently sane question. And exactly the right question to ask.

You've got to start by identifying what's not working – what doesn't feel right – so you can move out of stuck and right into happy.

Let's say you're stuck in your career. You've been in the same job with the same group for five, ten, fifteen years. You've got the system wired. You know where the bodies are buried. You've got the routine knocked.

And you are bored out of your freakin' mind.

First, identify what's not working. You've probably got pages to write on that one. Am I right? But then you start to say, "Well, yeah, but who else would pay me what I make here", or "Well, yeah, but I'd have to start over and wouldn't know anything", and maybe even, "Well, yeah, but it's not really that bad."

For those of you who have such big "buts", let me challenge you to look at your situation in a new way, with one more question: Did you get what you came for?

When you took the job, what did you want? Why did you take it in the first place? Because you needed the money? Because you could pick up certain skills? Because you could work with specific people? Because of prestige? Because it was the only job open?

And now, five, ten, fifteen years down the road, have you gotten what you came for? Have you met that initial objective? In spades?

Then maybe the reason you're stuck and bored and not as happy as you could be is because you've actually done what you set out to do. And the task at hand is to set new objectives and figure out if you can achieve them where you are – or if you have to find a new place to do what now needs doing in your life.

We human beings are designed to learn and grow and, believe it or not, be happy. And if your career has become like a bad habit, a routine that no longer gets the results you intended, then now is the time, and this is the place, to start making changes.

The Expectations Of Others

Shannon does a great job at work. Everybody says so. Her performance reviews are always "Exceeds Expectations" and she's been steadily promoted to a position of major responsibility.

So, why isn't she happy? She'll tell you she's burned out. She has no personal life. She has no time. She can't think. She forgets the birthdays of friends. She's productive at work, but still very, very stuck in a life that doesn't fit quite right.

What would she like? "I guess I would say, 'Peace' — time to hang with my friends. Time to maybe even have a boyfriend. Time to do quilting (which I love). Time to play with my nieces and nephews. Time to work out and get healthier. Time to do a really good job, too."

What's keeping her from that vision of a life? I ask her about her job and her eyes get glassy. "I work 10-12 hour days, probably six days a week," she says. "But there's always so much to do."

Any way she could delegate, or get more staff to help?

She pauses. "Well, I *could* try that, but I'm afraid I won't find anyone as committed as I am," she says. "I have pretty high expectations for others."

Hmmmn. I sense an avenue for exploration. I ask, "Shannon, what's 'success' mean to you?"

After a bit of hemming, hawing, inner cheek chewing and stolen glances toward the ceiling, Shannon says, "Success is not disappointing others, I guess. When I'm successful, I'm meeting the expectations of others."

"So," I start. "Other people get to decide how successful Shannon will be, and you have do what they say? You have no role in that? Because that's kinda what I hear you saying."

Tears well in Shannon's eyes. "I never thought about it that way," she says quietly.

"You can have a life of your own design, Shannon. It is possible. But you have to figure out what's most important to you and live by that, rather than accepting that assignment from others."

We take a look at Shannon's underlying fears and beliefs and began the process of eliminating and revising those that don't fit with the life Shannon would like to live.

It comes down to that idea Shannon has — that success means meeting the expectations of others. Is there another way to cast that sentence in a way that allows Shannon to get the life she wants to live? After some poking and prodding, we come up with:

"I am successful when I meet my *own* expectations."

Which is true. One of the best pieces of advice I ever received was from (shout out here) my friend Grey Terry. In a very difficult period of my life, Grey looked me in my perpetually red-rimmed eyes and said, "Michele, just do things today you can be proud of a year from now."

It was in my power, then, to have the expectation that I would face a great challenge as a person of integrity, responsible and respectable, a person of honor. And have my actions flow from these values. As a result, there's very little

I regret having done from that time of my life. Which is quite nice.

Shannon came to see that she, too, has the power to make and set her own expectations for how she will be in the world — that she will make time for the things that nourish her whole life, such as relationships, interests, exercise and a healthy diet.

Attempting to live by the expectations of others merely held her back. Now, she feels free.

And you? How do you feel?

A New Normal

You want to know how to change.

You want to know how to serve your priorities and your values.

You want to know how to do stuff differently.

I know you want this, because you've told me. You say, "Why do I keep facing the same stuff all the time? Why can't I do things differently?"

Well, how about this: When normal's not working for you, just make a new normal.

Meredith is unhappy in her work. She has a boss who says one thing and does another, and the ground is always shifting beneath her feet. Her normal is stressful, unpleasant, unhappy and needs to change. She knows this.

However, there's this issue of the economy, and her deep-seated belief that she should be able to turn the situation around, and that she shouldn't walk away from a challenge, and that maybe she's doing something really, really wrong and there's no job that would be any different.

Her normal sucks.

But the way she's looking at the prospect of a new normal equally sucks.

Unless...

Unless she can change just one thing. One tiny little thing. Toward a new way of being. Toward a new perspective. Toward a new normal.

Like, maybe, starting with a difficult conversation with her mercurial boss. Maybe, just maybe, calling him out on his inconsistencies. In a productive and collegial way, of course. By doing this one little thing, she'll shift her quiet, don't rock the boat, please-please-like-me normal into something a little stronger, a little prouder, a little better.

A new, happier, normal.

One area many clients have difficulty with is having difficult conversations. Does just reading that make your teeth grind? OK, difficult conversations are… difficult. Speaking up can be hard. Saying something that might, possibly hurt someone's feelings is so scary that many of us avoid saying anything.

And we internalize those icky emotions and end up all sick and unhappy and psychically smoooshed.

But when we create a new normal — a normal where we say what's hard when it's just a *little bit hard*, rather than waiting until until it's *big time hard* – we break the old patterns and create a new way of handling "hard".

Habits are tough to break, mostly because they feel so known and, therefore, feel rather safe. A new normal can seem impossible to get, because we're so familiar with what we've got.

Got to open your eyes to the possibilities, darlings, and dare to live a new normal. Because the payoff is big. The payoff is a life of your own design, doing things you like doing, with people you enjoy.

Change is possible, and good. Happiness is attainable. Hey, happiness — it's your new normal.

Would You Like Fries With That?

During my senior year in high school, it became glaringly evident that my need for hip huggers and puka shells exceeded my parents' willingness to underwrite my wardrobe.

It was clear that I needed a job.

One crisp autumn day, I walked into the fast food restaurant closest to school – a Roy Rogers, then owned by Marriott – and asked if they were hiring. I imagine I was wearing jeans with huge bell bottoms. I may have had a plaid shirt on. I was likely wearing either desert boots or Famolare Wave Sole shoes.

I was totally rocking the fashion. Which is why I was looking for a job in the first place.

The manager, a woebegone man who'd seen many a late night and too few an early morning, looked me over, head to toe, and wearily asked,"What do you do over at the high school?"

"Well," I chirped. "I'm President of the Student Union, on the Superintendent's Advisory Committee, in the ski club, in the drama club, and I've applied for early admission to Virginia Tech."

I was hired on the spot, and given a schedule and a uniform.

Roy Rogers was a Western-themed fast food restaurant, so my uniform consisted of a calico skirt, a white peasant-type blouse and a red and white cowboy hat.

Which totally offended my fashion sensibilities. And since the restaurant was across the street from my high school, I was continually embarrassed to be seen by classmates who came in for a tasty Double-R-Bar burger.

But Marriott offered a terrific training program. Believe it or not, I use what I learned then every single day.

- I rotate my stock – when I go to the grocery store, the new can of diced tomatoes goes behind the old so I'm always using the oldest stuff first.
- I know when to flip – my hamburgers come out medium every time.
- I know how to listen to customers and what they want.

And I know how to do suggestive selling. Which is when you ask, "Would you like fries with that?" or, since our Roy Rogers fries came in particular packaging, "Would you like a 'holster' of fries?" [Yes, the large fries were served in a cardboard gun holster. What can I say? It was a different time.]

I mention suggestive selling for a reason.

News reports out this week indicate that the real U.S. unemployment rate stands at 17.5 percent:

In all, more than one out of every six workers — 17.5 percent — were unemployed or underemployed in October. The previous recorded high was 17.1 percent, in December 1982.

This includes the officially unemployed, who have looked for work in the last four weeks. It also includes discouraged workers, who have looked in the past year, as well as millions of part-time workers who want to be working full time. (New York Times, Nov. 6, 2009)

If you are out of a job, now is the time to do some suggestive selling.

In a regular economy, 70% of job openings are not even advertised and are filled by personal referral. In my experience, right now it seems that about 90% of jobs are filled that way – because if an organization can only hire one person, they want a sure thing. A personal referral from someone who knows you and has worked with you is testimony that you're smart, sharp and can do the work. With a meaningful personal referral, you will get you the interview, and probably the position.

To get the referral, you have to suggestively sell your contacts. You have to tell them what you want and how you can solve the pain of an employer. Because all job hires are made because someone, somewhere is in pain. There's the pain of work overload, there's the pain of work not getting done, there's the pain of opportunities missed.

There's always pain. Identify it, sell how you can solve it, and you will rise to the top of the list.

If you're working part-time, it's even more important to suggestively sell. Saying things like, "I noticed that XYZ is not getting done. I'd be happy to do it," is the perfect way to move into a full-time slot.

And remember. Every job in your past has contributed to the skill set you have now. Play up all of your talents to sell yourself. Just because you had a certain job title in your last position doesn't mean you are limited to only that kind of work. I'll bet there are a lot of things you can do. Even though I'm no longer "Pardner Of The Month" (March, 1978), I could walk in any fast food joint today and make a credible hamburger.

And know how to ask, as I was trained, "Would you like fries with that?"

༄

W-O-R-K (A Four Letter Word)

Time for a gut check. Do you like what you do?

You get up each morning and get ready for your day — what's that like? Are you eager? Procrastinating? Measured? Rushed? Let me ask you this: Are you happy at the prospect of going to work?

I imagine there's someone reading this right now who scoffs at the very idea. "Michele," this person wants to say, "work is work. You're not supposed to like it! Work's just something you do to pay the bills and get financial security so someday you can retire and do whatever you daggone well please."

Hmmn. So, let me get this straight. I am supposed to work for forty years at a job I detest just so I can retire and get the freedom I postponed? How in the world does this make sense?

But it's a widely held view. And it governs us in so many ways.

A friend lamented that her teenage son has no drive. No ambition. No idea of what he wants to do. He isn't interested in getting a summer job. My friend is contemplating grounding him unless he finds a job, any job. Doesn't matter what he does, just as long as he works.

"Why do you think he doesn't want to work?" she asked. Maybe it's because all he hears is his mom and his dad complaining about their own jobs. He looks at his father and sees a man who misses games, and assemblies, and sports banquets because of the demands of his job. Who's distracted and on his Blackberry when he is home. Maybe he sees a mom who's frazzled and frantically juggling all the family elements that make up the boy's entire universe — school, home, sports, friends.

With this kind of role model around work, who would want to get a job?

The secret to being happy is this: do more of what you like and are good at, and do less of what you dislike — even if you are good at it. I, for example, dislike spreadsheets. Especially spreadsheets regarding historical spending, actual spending and proposed spending. They give me a headache. However, despite the pounding in my head, I am good at deciphering those kinds of spreadsheets and can be an active participant in discussions about them.

However, if I had a job that was solely spreadsheets, I'd be a morose blob of bleah.

I know a woman who is an accountant and has been at the same job for fifteen years. She goes in each day, does her work, goes home. It's a blob of bleah. She knows she's not really happy, but she's competent and that's all work is about, right? When you probe, you find out that what she'd really like to do is teach. The idea of teaching math to kids makes her whole face light up. But, she'll tell you, how could she possibly take the pay cut?

And, I ask: What's the price of being happier?

Maybe not as much as you think. It's a funny thing. When you start to do more of what you love, so much shifts. Time and time again, I have seen people take a "pay cut" and live richer lives. Either they find they need less than they thought, or they find that their priorities shift and needing that expensive suit, that keeping-up-with-the-Joneses vacation, that nifty sports car — just not important. Those "things" were only used to fill the gap that happiness now fills.

Or they find that they get paid more than they ever expected. They get salary increases, and bonuses. If they own their own business, clients flood in. Why? Because they are on fire about doing what they love. People who are passionate about what they do attract business and opportunities.

Wouldn't you recruit a teacher that all the students, parents and faculty adored? Wouldn't you want an accountant who found beauty and joy in numbers? Wouldn't you hire a coach who loves what she does?

Work doesn't have to be a four letter word. When you live a life of your own design — doing what you love and are good at — you'll find that even work feels like fun. And each day is a joy. And your kids *can't wait* to get a summer job.

Finding A Job 2.0

You need a job. $4 Gas has come and gone in the rearview mirror. And milk is more expensive than gas! You really need a job. Like yesterday.

Helpful people are telling you that no one's hiring, times are tough, you might as well give up, yadda yadda yadda.

Depressing. Especially if you want a job in, oh, energy, banking, the car industry...

But let me fill you in on a little secret: jobs are open in other sectors and people are getting hired.

So, how do you find those open positions and get yourself in the interview pool? Use the tools I call "Finding A Job 2.0". Ready?

Think big. Big picture, that is. Take a really big picture look at your skills — it doesn't matter what the industry is, if you know how to manage people, you know how to manage people. Ditto for handling budgets, problem solving, strategic planning, program management and tons of other areas. Focus on your most transferable skills, and make these the backbone of your search.

Know what you want to do. I know, you need a job. Any job. But when you succinctly define what it is you can do, it makes it so much easier for other people to understand and help you. Develop your own "elevator speech" — two to three sentences that capture the essence of what you want. For instance, "I'm looking for an executive director or VP position at a non-profit working on green issues. I've worked in this field for fifteen years and really know the issues, and like managing people." I understand that completely, and can refer you to two or three people who can help you.

Network with people you know. Over 70% of jobs are filled by personal referral. That means your Christmas card list, cell phone directory, email contacts, alumni directory and community phone book are your most important tools. Go through these personal lists and identify people who are already in the field where you want to work. Contact them, give them your elevator speech and ask if they know of any openings. Even if they don't have an immediate lightbulb moment, you've planted a seed in their minds — they'll remember you the next time they hear about something that would be perfect for you.

Network with people you don't know. If a friend says, "You should really meet my friend Tom", then go see Tom. Worst case scenario? You'll meet a new friend. Best case? Tom will know of a job for you. You can also use LinkedIn, Facebook, alumni discussion boards. Consider these opportunities to expand the reach of your resume and bio. Word to the wise? You can spend more time "updating" your social marketing pages than you do working on your job search. Use your time wisely.

Morph your resume. Gone are the days when you had one resume that a printer typeset for you on ivory laid paper. Many resumes are scanned into a humungous database, so make certain the words you use are keywords recruiters will use to fill a position like the one you seek. If you're responding to a particular job opening, tailor your resume to that job. Use the same keywords they use in the job posting. Stress that you have the skills they seek. And feel free to alter your resume for the next opening you pursue.

Write thank you notes. Sure, it's a holdover tactic from Finding A Job 1.0, but, hey, don't fix what ain't broke! The number of people who write thank you notes by hand is dwindling, so you will stand out when you're one of the few who use this tactic. Plus, gratitude is a happy place to be. Expressing your gratitude will increase your overall happiness and keep you positive for your next job interview.

Searching for a job in uncertain economic times is... uncertain. But by employing 2.0 tactics, you can make your job search efficient, effective and maybe, just maybe, quick.

Smart Networking

WHEN THE GOING GETS TOUGH, THE TOUGH GET... IN touch with their networks.

"You mean, Michele, that with the economy in free fall, the best thing I can do is network?" Incredulity is to truth as ham is to... what? [easy now, that's just a SAT analogy flashback]

OK, 70% of jobs are filled by personal referral. So it only makes sense that when unemployment is rising, and the economy is falling, your circle of friends and acquaintances becomes your most important insurance policy. 'Tis true, the people who know and like to work with you can speak most eloquently on your behalf. It also never hurts to have such a gold plated circle of contacts that your boss can't possibly fire you.

Over at BettyConfidential.com, I hammer on the importance of networking. Kinda thought I was the Queen of Networking. Until I met Liz Lynch. She's the true Queen of Networking, poppets, and I bow deeply to her.

Liz has a new book you're going to want to read — *Smart Networking: Attract A Following In Person And Online* (McGraw-Hill, 2008) — and despite my pretensions toward her throne, I got to enter the presence of the Queen and ask a few questions.

How do you define networking, Liz? "So many people see networking as going to events and meeting new people, but my definition is much broader. I define a 'network' as a support system of people you can turn to for help, advice, ideas, and information. 'Networking,' then, is simply the process of building and maintaining that support system, and being able to tap into it when you need help."

I have quite a few clients who've found themselves unexpectedly out of a job. Happening all over the world, in many different sectors. When you have to find a job fast, I asked Liz, do you just scramble to find a job, any job, and forget about the network?

"Actually, quite the opposite," Liz said. "Building a network does take time, but **the good news is that everyone has a network already.** People we've worked with, gone to school with, live near, play tennis with, etc. When you really need to get something done, it's these people, your most raving fans, that you should turn to first. While they may not be in a position to hire you themselves, you can get valuable advice on your job search and some may even be able to introduce you to others in their network who work at companies you're interested in. If nothing else, having moral support in these tough times can help you maintain confidence."

I told Liz that I love to work with professional women who are re-entering the workforce. Many of them whine, I mean, express deep concern, that their network is stale and out-of-date. Liz suggested, "What's really great about networking now is **all of the online options that are available that you can do on your own time and without having to leave the house.** An at-home mom can start to build her online network on LinkedIn and Facebook, and connect with folks she already knows. That way she gets on the radar screens of her old colleagues and can reach out to them much more easily once she's ready to start exploring her options. She can also start a business blog where once a week she can comment on news and trends in her industry. This is important because once she gets into job mode again, hiring managers are going to Google her. When her blog comes up and they read her insights and wisdom, it might just tip the scales in her favor."

Some small business owners see people in the same line of work as competition. Is there any benefit from growing a network with your competitors, Liz? Quoth the Queen, "My general philosophy with life is that **there is more than enough to go around.** Do you want to turn business away just so your competitor can prosper? No. You don't need to sacrifice yourself or give away your trade secrets, but being open to cooperation leads to win-win-win opportunities, where 1+1 can equal 5.

"For example, I have great relationships with other networking experts, and I feature some of them in the book. Why would I do this? **Because it helps everybody.** Readers get the benefit of hearing other experiences. The experts get the benefit of exposure in an international book, and hopefully because they're in it, they'll be willing to recommend it to their friends, colleagues and customers."

See why Liz Lynch is the Queen of Networking?

From her vantage point upon her throne, I wanted to know what her own network has done for her. Liz told me, "It's amazing when I think of how much my network has come through for me, and writing the book helped me remember so many of those moments. When I first left corporate America in 2000 to start my own consulting business, **my network** gave me nearly all of my business those first two years. Some hired me directly, some referred me to people they knew, and some just listened and gave me input on how to position myself. More recently, I got my book deal with McGraw-Hill without an agent as a first-time author with one email to someone in my network.

"For those who might be thinking that I have magical people in my Rolodex, I don't. They're all very special to me, but they're not household names. **The reason they're willing to help me is because I've built the relationship to last and I've mastered the art of the ask**, two very important topics I cover in Smart Networking."

The trick to successful investing is to buy low and sell high. When others are out of the market, there are often great openings for the taking. The same is true with networking. When so many people hunker down in fear, you can invest in your network. You can organize a volunteer activity for a group, or arrange a happy hour, or a lunch. You can step up your email contacts, or jump on Twitter or Facebook, or LinkedIn, where staying on your network's radar screen is easy.

Invest in your network now, and someday, just maybe, you'll sit high upon your own throne as the King or Queen Of Connections.

Finally Un-Stuck

STUCK.

Don't know.

Can't decide.

Feels awful.

Stuck is a nerve-wracking place. And takes a ton of energy. So much energy, in fact, that it's hard to find the oomph to do anything other than be stuck.

People who are stuck often face some kind of big decision or life change. And they torment themselves with, "Is this the right choice? What if I make a mistake?"

That is the stuck place. Can't move forward for fear of doing something wrong, and can't go back due to the space-time continuum, so... stay stuck.

There's only one way to break through the muck and get un-stuck. And that is to reframe the question from, "Is this the right choice?" to "Am I choosing growth?"

Dr. Carol Dweck has written a terrific book on making this shift - it's called *Mindset*, (Ballantine Books, 2007) and reading it has really turned my head around and refined the way I coach.

Dweck's research shows that simply shifting to a growth mindset opens up the stuck places. Of course, you have to believe it's possible to learn and to grow. Think it's possible? Yeah, I do, too. In fact, I value learning and growth as life-long pursuits. Do you?

If so, then when faced with a choice, always choose the option that gives you the most growth.

Doesn't that feel easier?

The other half of the stuck factor is: "What if I make a mistake?"

Because we all know that making a mistake is the worst possible thing that can happen, right? Right?

When you're coming from a focus on growth, though, mistakes have a lot less weight. Why? Because even mistakes are a place for learning.

If you choose growth, you give yourself a way to judge whether what you're doing is working - you just ask, "Is it possible for me to grow? Am I growing right now?" So you take a job and six months later you are doing something other than what they hired you for and you are uncomfortably bored and disappointed. Did you make a mistake? Or did you just stop growing? How would it feel to tell a prospective employer that you took a job, the conditions changed and you realized you couldn't grow there? Would feel pretty clear and clean to me. How about you?

When you choose growth, sweetums, you always win. Why? Because even in a worst case scenario, you've learned something. Something that will allow you to do better next time.

OK, I will address the elephant in the room which frequently factors in stuckness - "What will other people think?" That's a powerful mindset. And it's easy to say, "Well, I don't care what anyone else thinks", isn't it? But much harder to act in a way that runs counter to the beliefs of our families, our friends and our community of peers.

In a growth mindset though, my growth is my responsibility, and my commitment to myself. And if I am fully committed to my growth, then I can also be open and fully committed to yours. Which shifts the question from "What will other people think?" to "What will I think?" And removes another big stuck spot.

If you're stuck, I'm telling you, all you need to do is make a simple choice. Just choose to grow.

༄

The Integrity Thing

I've talked about how to get *Finally Un-Stuck* - remember?

"People who are stuck often face some kind of big decision or life change. And they torment themselves with, 'Is this the right choice? What if I make a mistake?' That is the stuck place. Can't move forward for fear of doing something wrong, and can't go back due to the space-time continuum, so… stay stuck. There's only one way to break through the muck and get un-stuck. And that is to reframe the question from, 'Is this the right choice?' to 'Am I choosing growth?'"

So, we choose growth, and get un-stuck. But there's something else - something vital - to factor into your decision-making.

It's called integrity.

To me, integrity means I'm not going to lie, I'm not going to cheat, I'm not going to take advantage of anyone, I'm not going to allow anyone to take advantage of me. I will say what I mean, and mean what I say. I will do what I've promised to do.

You may have other elements surrounding your personal integrity - but if you don't, now's the time to get clear on them, pardner.

Because when you choose growth within the framework of integrity - *there is no way you can make a mistake.*

Want an example? Okie doke. Tom is offered a job working for his company's biggest competitor and marketplace rival. It's a big leadership job, and it feels like growth to Tom - exactly the kind of step up he's been looking for. The new company promises him a signing bonus (asks him to keep quiet about it) and then kinda asks if he can bring over his files on a particular innovation Tom has been overseeing at the old company.

Now, some people would say, "Sure, that's the way the game is played. He should absolutely bring everything to his new employer! What are you, Michele? Some kinda dope? This happens all the time."

Ah, yes, grasshopper, it does happen all the time. Especially with people who have lost touch with their own integrity. And that's why this is such an important moment for Tom - he can choose a new opportunity where he knows his integrity will be challenged, or say no and preserve something important to him.

I'm going to humor those who say, "Take the money and run, Tom!" Let's say he chooses to take the new job. A year later, where's Tom? Unhappy, compromised, constantly fudging the facts and lying to his team. He's miserable. And his former colleagues? He's lost them - they're still smarting from his conduct as he walked out the door. Day to day, he's struggling with the consequence of abandoning something really important to him - his integrity. It's crushing stress.

I've seen this sad scenario play out hundreds of times.

Remember this line from above? When you choose growth within the framework of integrity - *there is no way you can make a mistake.*

Well here's the corollary: Any opportunity that asks you to put your integrity aside *is most assuredly not a growth opportunity - and ultimately will be a mistake.*

There's a lot written these days about "Your Personal Brand" -hey, I've even written about it:

"...your own personal brand is really about living in alignment with your integrity and what's best about you. And when you're truly in alignment that way, life becomes easy." (*Your Personal Brand*, August 23, 2009)

Any of us can convince ourselves that nearly anything is a growth experience. The gut check, then, is seeing where the new opportunity lines up with your integrity. When you can grow while preserving your integrity, you are, indeed, making the absolute right choice.

༄

Love Your Work? (What Are You, Crazy?)

I GOT AN EMAIL THIS WEEK FROM A LOVELY 25-YEAR OLD reader - she asked:

"Since you work with a lot of professionals and others in the work force - what's your experience? How many people out there really love their jobs? I wonder if I was being too negative in thinking that there's no such thing as the perfect job or that I'll never just LOVE going to work every day. Any advice to thoughts along these lines?"

This is a great question, whether you're 25 and just launching your career, or if you're 55 and in the thick of your working life. Can't wait to answer it.

First of all, there seems to be a collective idea about The Plan. Know what I mean? The Plan goes like this: Do well in high school –> go to a great college –> go to law school/get a MBA/become a doctor –> get the perfect job.

And guess what? Doesn't always happen like that. Sorry to burst your balloon, kiddo. I read a story in the Washington Post that might be of interest - 22-year old Bekah Steadwell graduated from a competitive college - Oberlin - and is working two jobs as a cook while living at home with her parents. And her two college-graduate sisters. Her path is much different from the one we outlined above, huh?

The trick for Bekah and anyone else whose path did not go the way they planned - they couldn't get a job in their field, or worse, *got* a job and realized they didn't really want to do that kind of work - is to accept that their path is different, and that *it's not necessarily a bad thing.*

Perhaps the biggest hurdle is *accepting* that The Path is a myth - one which creates legions of quietly desperate anxious strivers in pursuit of the impossible. Because you could go to the very best schools in the world, achieve academic excellence, get a coveted job in a prestigious place - and absolutely hate what you are doing.

It happens.

So what do you do if you find yourself hating your job?

Here's what I tell my clients who find themselves in this fix - ask yourself four questions:

1. **What can I do all by myself to create a better work situation?** Could you break up the monotony by consciously doing things differently? Can you learn to manage difficult people?
2. **How can I shift my thoughts away from the negative, toward the positive, about this job?** Can you focus on the outcomes - like how, because of your job, you can afford that gym membership, or that trip? Can you seek to find the good?
3. **Have I ever been happy?** Look at past happy experiences and see if you can replicate any of the factors you loved back then into your current work. But if you've never been happy in any job, then there may be something you need to explore. See #4.
4. **Are there underlying issues I need to work out?** If you've had a series of unreasonable, demanding female bosses and you had an unreasonable, demanding mother, it doesn't take Dr. Freud to determine that

a bit of therapy might be in order. Really. Burying past ghosts is the single best path toward creating a happy now.

The first step in any situation that's not working is to look at yourself and make positive changes. And if you try, and you still can't find relief... then it's time to leave.

No matter what The Plan says.

༶

When Your Job Is A Soul-Sucking Hellhole

In the last essay, *Love Your Work? (What Are You, Crazy?)* we looked at how you can single-handedly turn around a difficult work situation. Yes, I said, "single-handedly." And I meant it - when you first look to yourself and change (for the good) what you can - then, you can absolutely, positively, single-handedly turn around a difficult situation. I've seen it too many times to doubt that it's a successful strategy.

And if you are doing the right thing, you are firmly in your integrity, and your work stays a soul-sucking hellhole, then... it's time to quit.

I wrote about *When To Quit* a couple of years ago (January 6, 2008). Come to think of it, I really liked that post. In it, I suggested:

"It's time to quit when the person you are becoming is someone you don't like. When you're in a job, and as a condition of employment you are expected to fudge facts, shift numbers and lie to customers, you become a person who fudges, shifts and lies. Is that who you want to be?"

And,

"It's time to quit when you find that you love having the problem more than the problem loves you. If you find yourself talking about the problem all the time, stewing and fretting, worrying about it, analyzing it, turning the problem over and over in your head - is that who you want to be? Is that how you want to use your energy?"

Now, let's just be honest right here. Some of us slip into a familiar and comfy place where we absolutely love using our energy stewing and fretting, worrying, analyzing. Why? Darlings, it's an artful dodge. What are we dodging? Why, fear, of course. We're dodging and dancing around the thing so many of us fear the most - fear of change.

We change-fearers expend all our energy mulling things over - which leaves us absolutely zero energy to do the thing we need to do most: *change something.* So, to snap out of the contemplative coma and get going, ask yourself these questions:

1. **In the past, when I've made a change like the one I'm contemplating now - what's been the outcome?** Look back, write it down. What's your change experience been like? How does that inform your actions right now? If you've been less than adept at change, what did you lack at the time? Can you shore that up this time?

2. **What scares me most about making a change right now?** I'm not kidding: Make a list. Then look at each item that scares you and say, "If that happens, then what?" Follow the trail right down to the thing that scares you most. Such as, "I will become the bag lady who lives in a shopping cart at Westmoreland Circle." Then decide: is that really possible? This approach puts many fears right where they belong - out of your way.

3. **If I make this scary change, how will I grow?** (remember *Finally Un-Stuck*, where we talked about the power of always choosing growth?)

4. **By staying where I am - do I like myself? Do I even want to like myself?**

That last one's a zinger, huh? But coming to terms with whether you'll ever allow yourself to truly *like* yourself - now there's a thought worth pursuing.

So let's say, for the sake of argument, that you have quieted your fears, you want to *feel* better and you want to *be* better. What do you do next?

You know me - I'll tell you to focus on your strengths, your passions, your priorities and your values. I'll tell you to network, network, network. I'll tell you to read *Finding A Job 2.0* about the new rules of finding a job.

I'll tell you to take a deep breath and get yourself unstuck. Because there's so much more to life than that soul-sucking hellhole where you work.

So much more.

༄

…
When Gifts Become Junk

Difficult people are so difficult.

Demanding, whiny, needy, unreasonable, unconscious, a pain in the butt, belligerent, jerk, fearful... I can go on. Bet you can, too. Some people just sap the energy from the room. Or are so negative and critical that being around them is never joyful. Don't you find your own mood shifting to match theirs? So what starts as a great day becomes a freak show. What a downer. Who wants to live like that?

So, you've got a Energy Sucking Black Hole Of A Person in your life. What do you do?

We are trained from childhood to always accept a gift even if it's like the fancy soap that I once received as a gift — and the soap had been used. Yes, I had been re-gifted. And the original gift card from the original giver was in the bottom of the box.

We've been told to graciously accept even gifts such as this and write a thoughtful, tasteful thank you note. Regardless.

Yet.

I have received gifts I cannot use. Don't want. Don't make sense. That really belonged to someone else. Sometimes these gifts reflect what other people think I should be, or should like, or should want. Which aren't gifts at all.

And these things clutter my life.

As I cleaned out a linen closet yesterday, I uncovered many presents I had been holding on to because they were gifts, afterall. And one is supposed to be grateful. So, I had stuffed them into a closet and they slowly turned into junk. Junk which is making its way to Goodwill later today.

Feel a metaphor coming at you?

OK, just because a person wants to give me a gift of… their negativity, their anxiety, their fear… I can simply say no thanks and let them keep it. Because if I accept their gift, I clutter up the linen closet of my life.

It really comes down to: if I spend my time and energy sharing their discontent and helping them live their life, when do I have time to live my own?

People come to me for help with the difficult people they encounter at work. And often it comes down to not setting boundaries, which is hard for so many of us. A co-worker sits down to "vent" and we feel the need to help. But we get drawn into office politics, gossip and drama — which keeps us from doing what we want to do with our lives and careers.

All theoretical I know. So I will be practical. We really need to do is reflect their "gift" right back to them. Place it squarely in their hands — because it's their gift in the first place.

And you do that by saying, "Wow, sounds tough. What do you plan to do about it?"

That's how you do it. Kindly, respectfully, with boundaries intact. And then you get on to living your own life.

Make Your Own Thanksgiving

This week I've been thinking about money.

And how so many people get all weird and wobbly when it comes to talking about it. Asking for it. Having it at all.

And it's interesting that they way our parents and grandparents handled money probably affects the way we handle money. I think about the woman whose immigrant parents struggled and sacrificed and lived in poverty. And now, even though she makes a million dollars a year, she hoards paper towels and soup... just in case.

Or the guy whose dad was a dreamer and a schemer. When they had money, they spent it – lavish dinners, fancy trips, stylish clothes. And when they had no money, they fantasized about how they'd spend it once it came back. Today, this guy has no savings and wonders what happens to his cash.

A couple of months ago I wrote *When Gifts Become Junk* – just because someone gives you a gift, like a legacy around money, you don't have to take it.

It's kind of like Thanksgiving.

I remember the first time I had to cook Thanksgiving on my own. I planned to carefully replicate the traditional family menu, but then ran into a little blip. Where my family had bread-and-oyster dressing, heavy on the sage, his family had cornbread dressing with plenty of celery and onion. My family was mashed potatoes, his was rice. Ours was brown gravy. His had hard-boiled eggs floating in a yellow gravy.

We each had our own idea of What Thanksgiving Is and What One Must Consume So It Is Truly Thanksgiving. Compromise felt like loss.

Oh, I come by the feeling of What It Should Be quite naturally – another family legacy. I remember my mother preparing Thanksgiving when I was a child. She looked at our loaded table and would always say, "You know, my grandmother would have chicken and dumplings, ham, turkey, fried chicken, and four different kinds of pie…this just doesn't seem like Thanksgiving to me." The fact that we had ham and turkey and three pies – never lived up to what Thanksgiving Should Be.

What a struggle. It's the tension between fantasy and reality, really. It's the tightrope of being present right here and now, and living in a storied and maybe flawed recollection of a "better time." It's an oppressive and unrealistic burden because the past you're trying to match was probably not as wonderful as you recall. It probably wasn't any more happy than you can make today.

So to be firmly here in the present, and living a happy life, there comes a point when you simply choose to make your own Thanksgiving.

Take a look at the heritage of your forebears and decide what you want to consciously take forward with you in your own life. It is absolutely OK – hey, it's more than OK, it's imperative — to decide whether you want to continue with the tiny marshmallows on the top of the super sweet potatoes, or go a bit healthier and replace that traditional dish with, oh, steamed broccoli.

You create your own traditions, not because what your parents and grandparents did was wrong. It may have been really right. For them. At that time. But now, it's your life. You can create your own way of being in the world, darling, because you are you – not them.

Look at the legacies gifted to you by your parents and grandparents — around money, around relationships, around body image, around holidays – and decide: "Is this what I want for myself? Does this make me happy, or give me stress?"

If a tradition works for you, and makes you very, very happy – then keep it. If a tradition feels like a heavy obligation, and makes you very, very stressed – then it's time to lovingly let that relic go.

Feel free to make your own menu, and it will be your own Thanksgiving. Every single celebratory day.

౿

Money Changes Everything

Let me shoot straight with you.

Most of your biggest problems stem from fear.

And most of your biggest fears boil down to money.

Will I have enough?

Will I have enough to do all the things I should do? Buy the things I should buy?

Will I fit in with my peers if I don't have $150 jeans or regular Botox injections or trips to Disney World?

What if I have too much, and don't fit in? What if I become everyone's piggybank?

What if I lose everything? What would people think?

We place so much meaning on money.

What I'm paid reflects my value to society.

If you give me money, you must like me.

Money is the way to get the power to do what you want.

And there's the negative about money.

People with money are unhappy, egotistical jerks.

Money changes everything. For the worse.

These fundamental, underlying, limiting ideas around money don't really help you - they only serve to hold you back. You don't ask for the raise, because you're afraid you'll find out what your boss really thinks about you. Which is - you fear - not much.

Or you decline to negotiate your child support agreement because you fear you'll be reminded that your ex disliked you enough to end your marriage.

It's a potent cocktail of emotion. And some of you have ordered a double. On the rocks.

But, believe me, money can be simple. It can be easier. Know how?

Do this: Shift to seeing money as a tool. Just a tool. Not a referendum on you as a person. Or your value to society. Or your desirability.

Swap out your troubling money thoughts for this: "Money is a tool that will allow me to do things in support of my priorities."

Of course, you need to know your priorities. And be very clear on them. And make sure they're your priorities, and not the priorities of your parents, your grandparents, your peers or any of the Kardashian sisters.

Because, in the long run, taking care of your financial health is the ultimate expression of self-care.

When I take good care of my financial health, I am taking good care of me. And of my priorities, goals and intentions.

And when I am free of limiting, negative, fearful attitudes toward money, I can easily ask my clients to pay me, or ask my boss for a raise. I can make wise purchases and investments that support me and where I want to go. When I am clear, I am the best advocate for myself.

When I stop operating from fear around money, I naturally move to living in comfort with money. I go from "can't" to "can." I move from lack to abundance, spontaneously.

It's not that money changes everything, honey. It's your attitude around money that truly changes things. Let it be for the better.

༄

More On Money

Money Changes Everything got a lot of attention. Comments, tweets - many of you wrote me directly to share your own personal fears around money.

I figure I hit a nerve.

Money is a hot button issue for a bunch of reasons, and we talk about some of them in a class I lead on the subject. First, money is shrouded in secrecy. Remember when you were a kid? Did you know how much your dad made? Or how much your mom brought in? Did you know what your family's mortgage payment was? Or how much it cost to load up the station wagon and drive to the Grand Canyon that long, hot summer?

Of course you didn't.

One doesn't talk about money.

And how did that set you up to handle your own money? Did you have knowledge, and experience, and a context for your own spending? Your savings? Your investing?

Did secrecy allow you to stand up and ask for money? No, I'm guessing it didn't. Which is why you often find out too late that you are paid forty percent less than the guy in the cube right next to yours - and you do exactly the same work with the same result.

There's also a ton of meaning assigned to money. Many of us think, "When I am paid $X, I will have it made." But when we get paid $X, we still don't have it made. It's like the guy who thought plastic surgery would change his life. Truth? He had the same old troubles and worries - he just had a new face.

And we have so many ideas about money - ideas like, "Don't keep your money in a bank. Banks cheat people like us." Or, "Stocks and insurance are just for rich people." Or, "My family has never had two nickels to rub together."

The conflict comes in when we do have a bank account, stocks, insurance and a savings account. It's pretty challenging to go up against all those beliefs people you love held dear.

But that's exactly what you need to do to get your money mindset in order.

I love when people make big discoveries about themselves. That light bulb pops up over their head, there's a gleam in their eye, they exhale three decades of stress out slowly - it's a truly wonderful moment.

But there's a step that comes after discovery. It's asking yourself, "OK, now I get it. My ideas about banks are really my grandmother's ideas about banks. **What do I want my own idea about banks to be?**"

To set yourself free, you have to own your own ideas, born of your own experiences.

So if you want the secrecy to stop, stop it. Sit down with your kids and go over a budget - with income and expenses. Tell them there are some things a family shares with each other, and that you trust them enough to share something important. How do you think that will set them up to be successful, independent, financially secure adults?

Pretty well, I'm thinking.

And meaning? To tell you the truth, whatever you think you'll do when you "have it made" - you can do right now. Want to be in a position to give back? Donate blood. Officiate a softball game. Mentor a kid. Want to relax and be less worried about money? Take charge of your finances. Completely understand where you're spending and decide to do it in a way that brings out the best in you. Want to have stuff you love? Love the stuff you have.

When you take care of your financial health, you **will** have it made. Because you'll feel better about yourself and your life.

Which is the whole point.

༄

How To Tell A Story

STORIES ARE SUCH POWERFUL THINGS. PEOPLE CERTAINLY love listening to stories being told and telling stories themselves.

Most of all, folks seem to adore telling stories *about* themselves, which I find very revealing.

When someone tells me a story that goes something like this: "I can't _____ because _____," or "I'm not _____ because _____," I know they're stuck. They're probably telling a story about themselves that once may have been true but no longer really works. The old story holds them back, yet a new story seems unwritten and, perhaps, unwriteable.

Hey, want to look at your personal narrative and figure out if the story you're telling about yourself is actually moving you toward something, or holding you back?

I sure do. Ready?

So what is the story you tell about yourself? [reader does a spewing spit take] "I don't tell a *story*, I just live my life," the reader says with indignation.

Uh-huh.

Take out a piece of paper and make two columns. Title the first column: Now Words. In that column write words to describe your life as it is right now.
Bored
Stressed

Stuck
Routine
Honest
Kind
Generous

Write as many describing words as you'd like. Then, title the second column, "Future Words" and start writing words that describe the life you *want* to have. You may carry Now Words into the Future Words column. For instance:

Honest
Kind
Generous
Happy
Fun
Loving
Creative

Now, here's where you change your personal narrative. Start consciously using your Future Words in your day-to-day life, and start taking actions that bring those words to life. So, if "creative" is a part of your future, what can you do today to create? Be very specific: "I can write 10 pages. I can solve a problem. I can work in my garden. I can throw a pot. I can paint." Name your creative thing, then go ahead and do it.

We can all make lists, friends. But not all of us are adept at putting our energy in the game and actually *doing*. All it takes to re-write your personal narrative is awareness of what you want, backed up by purposeful action.

When you pair that up, you'll find — pretty soon — that you're telling a new, happier story. I promise you, it will be one you'll enjoy telling so much more than the old version. Oh, and you'll be living a happier, more successful life.

That's my story, and I'm… well, you know the rest.

∽

3 Ways To Get Out Of Your Own Way

People ask me how I write these columns every week. Well, I'll tell you: sometimes I have a plan, and sometimes the plan goes out the window in favor of an idea that keeps popping up.

If it keeps popping, I start writing.

And so it was this week. The thing that kept popping up? "Michele, how can I get out of my own way?"

Excellent question. Good news: I've got three ways for you to start.

First, figure out why you're making things harder than they have to be. Is it because someone once told you that anything worth getting requires a struggle? The Anxious Struggler zeitgeist runs through popular culture. Boy meets girl, boy wants girl, boy triumphs over adversity (and her initial disinterest), boy gets girl. See how the struggle pays off there? {except, of course, in the TV Show "The Bachelor", where it appears a boy can go through the whole "get the girl" scenario, dump her and get another girl, thereby adding to the struggle, emotion and pathos. I'm just sayin'.}

In my experience, people often create more of a struggle than there really needs to be just to satisfy widely held cultural values around struggle. When, in fact, the things that are often best for us are those things that come easily. In a spiritual context, many faiths talk about allowing, submitting and being open. When you are open to the gifts already there for you, you don't need to struggle. You can just receive. Nice idea, huh?

So, to really get out of your own way, drop the struggle and take the most fluid, joyful, easy path. Which leads to the second tip...

Center in your strengths. You may have heard me say this once or twice before...but if you are an excellent writer, why work in a field where you never write? If you are great with people, why work solo in a lab? If you can sing, why not do it?

"Nobody will pay me for what I'm good at," is something I often hear. Which is an excellent example of someone being in his own way. Your expertise is always valued. But first it has to be valued by you. It's funny that what comes easily to us is often the thing we discount the most. Sure, to live in your strengths you may have shift the way you benchmark your success. If you go from being a Wall Streeter to running a hospice center, you will probably take a pay cut. But you will definitely get the bonus of doing something that matters and has meaning. Priceless.

When you center every day in your strengths, you are absolutely in the flow. Life is effortless. Plus, it's really, really fun.

Third thing you can do to get out of your own way? Listen to your intuition. OK, I know that many of us are Just The Facts, Ma'am kinda folks. And you all are rarely in your own way, if you want to know the truth, because you see the facts and decide and move on. It's us intuitive people who think and re-think, and mull and ponder, and see a zillion options and maybes and might-possibly-happens and get in our own way because it can't possibly be that easy, can it, I mean, got a minute to let me run this by you, what do you think?

Sound familiar?

Did to me. Until I did one little exercise. I wrote down every time I'd had an intuition about something and turned out to be right. I also wrote down every time I'd had intuitive guidance and did the opposite of what my gut told me. Figured out the consequences of those choices right then and there and realized: My gut is almost always right. Like 95% right.

So, now, I stay out of my own way primarily by listening to my gut and letting it lead me. Sure, sometimes I give myself the 24 Hour Rule: I wait 24 hours and if the gut feeling is still there, I go ahead and do whatever needs doing. If, in 24 hours, I feel icky — I don't do whatever. I just move on.

And, I'm out of my own way a lot of the time. But it's not just me — it's plenty of other people, too, who manage to stay out of their own way. They do just three simple things. 1.) Challenge your thoughts about the value of struggle. 2.) Center in your strengths. 3.) Listen to your gut.

When you're out of your own way, you'll find that great stuff will happen. You'll have happy effortlessness in your life.

∽

What's Your Why?

LET'S FACE IT. IT'S A SCARY WORLD OUT THERE. PEOPLE are losing their homes, and losing their jobs. In fact, unemployment in the U.S. hasn't been this widespread since 1974.

Think – babies born in 1974 are 35 years old today. Probably married. Probably a couple of kids. Couple of credit cards. Car payments. Mortgage. Bills.

Thirty-five year olds have no frame of reference for what's going on now. My guess is they figured home values would always go up, as would salaries, bonuses and retirement plans. When up, up, up turns to down, down, down – it's a frightening, unsettling experience.

Even folks with jobs who pay their mortgages on time are feeling beseiged, as if at any minute they could be in trouble, too. We feel powerless. The rug has been pulled out from underneath, or is about to be tugged violently. What's the purpose of life if you lose everything you've worked your whole life to achieve? Where's the meaning in that?

This week I picked up an old favorite to re-read – Viktor Frankl's book *Man's Search For Meaning*. Frankl, an Austrian psychiatrist, was imprisoned in Auschwitz and Dachau, and he writes eloquently about his harrowing experiences in the death camps. It was through unimaginable suffering that Frankl was able to find meaning not only in his life, but to fully understand how others find meaning in theirs.

Frankl suggests that meaning and purpose is derived from having a *why*. Why live? Why suffer? Why keep putting one foot in front of the other? In the camps, Frankl discovered, survival of the inmates was completely dependent on having a *why*: "Whenever there was an opportunity for it, one had to give them a why – an aim – for their lives, in order to strengthen them to bear the terrible *how* of their existence."

Frankl says our *why* is always one of three things: doing something, loving someone, or rising above yourself by turning tragedy into triumph.

Now, I have to say this. Losing your job is not the same as being in Dachau. Even in 1974, people ultimately found new jobs. Losing your home? Not Auschwitz. But these are certainly tough times. To survive, you have to know your own personal *why*.

And if you're stuck, struggling, hurting, depressed... you especially need to get in touch with your *why* and let it guide your life.

Ask yourself, what's my reason for being here? Is there something you need to accomplish? Someone whose life you cherish? Is your *why* to parent your children into independent adulthood? Is it to love and support your spouse? Is it to take this very difficult time – to be willing to lose everything you've worked for – and emerge stronger, more confident, and wiser?

All of these are excellent *whys*. And when you have your *why* fixed firmly in your mind, you can do more than endure. You can move forward and thrive.

You not only *can*. You *will*.

You.

A FEW YEARS AGO I WROTE ABOUT HOW MANY MESSAGES we get everyday not-so-subtly telling us that there is some pill, some diet, some program, some magical thingy, that will allow us to lose weight, find love, de-clutter and save money. The sassy essay was so popular it became the title of first book, Lose Weight, Find Love, De-Clutter & Save Money: Essays on Happier Living.

But as I said then and I'll say now, the key to making changes in your life is not in some external thingy — it's a totally internal thingy. It's you. When you like yourself and support yourself and do good things for yourself, you will be at the right weight, you will be in love, your clutter will be what you want it to be, and you will be financially healthy.

Easier said than done?

Yes. Exactly.

The key to liking yourself is in the words you use. Use the right words the right way and the world becomes your oyster. Unless you don't like oysters, in which case, the world becomes your... playground. And if you don't like playgrounds... well, what do you like?

And that's precisely it. If you can be conscious of every time you say negative words, like "don't", "no", "can't", "won't", and "shouldn't", you'll see just how negative your self-talk is. Which may be just the thingy that's holding you back.

To move forward, teach yourself — every single time you say a negative word — to immediately turn it around to something positive. So, "I don't want to work for an egocentric jerk" leads right into "but I do want to work for someone smart with a good sense of humor."

Instead of focusing your energy on what you won't do (negative), you are shifting to what you will do (positive). Which allows you to see possibilities rather than limits. Which makes happy instead of stuck. Which means that when we're not blinded by negativity, we can open our eyes and see good things happen.

There's another language tic that deserves shifting. It's when we disassociate from ourselves by using the word "you". As in when someone's explaining their job and they say, "You want to do a good job and everything, but you're concerned that you'll get taken advantage of because the boss is a bully."

You've heard this before. You've probably even said it yourself. More than once.

And maybe we human beings talk this way because what we're saying is so close to our hearts. Or feels really emotional. So we get a little separation by using "you" rather than "I". Or maybe we are trying to make some connection with the person we're talking with, as in "Please tell me you've had this experience, too." Or maybe we're just so distant from our real selves that we can't claim our individuality by using a singular pronoun.

Which is kind of sad.

But think about the power if you were to say, "I want to do a good job and everything, but I'm concerned that I'll get taken advantage of because the boss is a bully." Wow. Now you're talking. Now you're claiming. Now, rather than some vague "you", it's a specific "I". It's "me".

And I count. And I matter. And I am claiming how I feel and what I know. And what I'm going to do now.

I know for a fact that when I took these two steps — stating positively what I will do, and using "I" rather than "you" to refer to myself — my life began to be my own. Things got easier. Life got better. On the Happiness Meter, I was often at 11 on a scale of 1 to 10. {OK, what's a blog post without a Spinal Tap reference, I ask you?}

And the promise is there for you, too. Be conscious of where your language is negative and disassociated from the "I", and shift it. I know **you** can do it. The world will be your oyster. Or your playground. It's your choice.

༄

More Than Anything

I dunno. Maybe it's just me. Or most of my clients. But I have a feeling it could be you, too.

A little exhausted, frazzled, distracted, uncertain? Sound like you? Sounds a teensy-tiny bit familiar to me.

So let me ask us a question:

"What do you want more than anything right now?"

Stop. You have an immediate answer, don't you? That's your gut talking to you.

And you immediately reject your gut, because what it's saying isn't politically correct, or is hugely inconvenient, or it's not what you're *supposed* to want.

Am I right?

But, let me tell you that if you want to feel better — more passionate, happier, alive — you have to pay attention to that poor little rejected feeling. Because the first glimmer is the key to unlocking whatever it is that's holding you back.

If what you want right now is: a rest, a new job, peace and quiet, a boyfriend, a girlfriend, no friends, children, your children to be quiet, your children to get the hell out of the house — take a deep breath and hold the idea of getting what you want in your mind. Believe you've actually achieved it. You're really living it.

How's that feel?

Blissful? I'll bet it does.

Then, my friend, perhaps you should consider pursuing that which you want more than anything. *Right now.*

Which might mean something might have to change.

Beth recently asked me, "Does all change start with a crisis? Cuz it sure seems like it." I answered her with, "There seem to be three ways that change gets started. In the first instance, there's some sort of crisis that's external — the shock of a sudden death, or an accident, or your spouse suddenly announces he's been seeing a 19 year old pole dancer named Tiffani. It comes, often without warning, from outside sources.

"Another kind of change comes from an internal source — realizing you have to start being yourself, for example, or an uncomfortableness with the status quo — and that's the second way. It comes from inside you, and probably doesn't involve Tiffani. The third way is perhaps more subtle — it's change that you're only aware of after it's done. Think of it this way — it's when you study and practice a language and then one day realize you're *thinking* in that new language."

So, let's all think in a new language. The old language may look like this, "I want everyone to think I'm a great, involved mother, so asking the kids to go outside to play would mean I'm a failure", and the new language is, "I will be a better, rested, more engaged mother if I can get a little time to myself."

The old language may be, "Everyone expects me to be a CPA for the rest of my life," and the new language may be, "I really want to be a park ranger."

The old language may be, "If I show how much I want an intimate partner, I'll look desperate," and the new language is, "I can only get what I want if I'm completely honest with myself and others."

So, be completely honest. What do you want more than anything right now?

And what does that tell you about what you need to do next?

∽

Loving Change

It's funny. I am usually the cock-eyed optimist who writes about how to create more happiness and joy in your life and your work.

I often tell you to focus on what's working, and do more of that, and do less of the stuff that drains you or makes you unhappy.

I will tell you that's The Secret of Life.

However.

Today, I'm telling you that sometimes, to make a change, you have to dwell in what really stinks.

Today, I'm suggesting that you have to wade right in and bathe in what's worst about your situation to really make a change.

You know, maybe it's human nature to hate change. Maybe it's human nature to gaze at the bright side and tell ourselves that it's really not so bad, this is what we need to do, maybe something else would be worse. Or harder. Or suck even more than the sucky thing we are already acquainted with.

But when you're exhausted, or sick, or heavier than you need to be... Or when you have a short fuse, or are constantly on edge, or hate going into your office...

Then you've gotta start loving change.

It's kind of like making your grandmother's favorite casserole. The recipe calls for sour cream, butter, cream of mushroom soup, cream cheese and cheddar. You love your grandmother, and you love her cooking. Brings back memories. But eating sour cream, butter, cream of mushroom soup, creamed cheese and cheddar all baked together is not how you want to live your life today.

To change the recipe to suit the way you want to eat today, you make changes. Substitutions. Like using chicken broth, herbs, more protein. Sure, it's not grandma's recipe exactly. It might taste kind of like hers, but really – it's yours now.

You know I have the idea that we each have 100 units of energy to spend each day. Yesterday's are gone, and tomorrow's belong to tomorrow. All you've got is 100 to use today. And if you have created day-after-day which calls for 120, you've got a problem.

It's just like having too much dairy and fat in a recipe.

Something's gotta go.

This is something that I've begun to realize about my own life. There are tactics, approaches, habits, ways of being, that worked for me as a coach, say, five years ago, but don't particularly work for me today.

So, I'm going to let them go.

I'll admit it – I feel a little uncertain about the changes I'm going to make. Will they work? Will I be happy? Will I make the revenue I want to make?

Truth? I don't know. I could be making a mistake.

But.

The alternative – not making a change – feels like continuing to eat food that's satisfying, but not really supportive of the way I really want to live.

You're probably wondering what I'm going to do.

Right?

I'm going to do less one-on-one coaching, and focus on groups, workshops, retreats and speaking. I'm talking about having maybe five individual clients. That seems about right to me.

And it's a big shift. Because right now? I've got about 20 individual clients. And the paradigm for many coaches is a plethora of clients. For many coaches, that's their bread and butter. The source of most of their revenue. And I'm letting that go.

Kinda scary.

What I want is more time to create. What I want is more time to focus. What I want is a few of the absolutely right clients to work with very closely. And I want a bunch of the absolutely right people to work with in groups.

Because I have a priority around creating. Which is hard to do when you're flat out. So I am reallocating my energy units so I can have the space, and time, to create.

Maybe you've created a recipe for your life that once worked, but isn't working so well for how you want to live your life today. If so, wade right in and figure out what ingredients need to be swapped out. Figure out how to make a satisfying dish out of healthier stuff. And love that change.

Change: Tastes great. And, less filling.

Change Or Die

Being stuck stinks. You're stuck when you know you can't stay where you are but you don't exactly know where to go. It's like running on a treadmill covered in molasses - slow and sticky. And you're forever running in place.

Why do we get stuck at all? Why can't we rational human beings simply decide to do this, that or the other thing and get a move on?

Ah, if only it were that simple.

A few years ago I read a fascinating article in Fast Company magazine called "Change or Die", and it's been really helpful in so many ways. It gave me insight into something important: people stay stuck in situations that aren't good for them because they can't see how making a change will lead to anything positive.

Let's look at wellness. The bulk of medical expenses come from five lifestyle habits — smoking, drinking, eating, stress and not enough exercise. Most doctors tell patients "make changes in these areas, or you will die". But in a few months or years the patient goes back to the bad old habits that brought on the trouble in the first place. We know what's good for us, but we just don't do it. Why?

"Change or Die" cites the work of Dr. Dean Ornish, who has achieved remarkable long-term results by taking a different approach with heart patients:

"Doctors had been trying to motivate patients mainly with the fear of death, he says, and that simply wasn't working. For a few weeks after a heart attack, patients were scared enough to do whatever their doctors said. But death was just too frightening to think about, so their denial would return, and they'd go back to their old ways.

"The patients lived the way they did as a day-to-day strategy for coping with their emotional troubles. 'Telling people who are lonely and depressed that they're going to live longer if they quit smoking or change their diet and lifestyle is not that motivating,' Ornish says. 'Who wants to live longer when you're in chronic emotional pain?'

"So instead of trying to motivate them with the 'fear of dying,' Ornish reframes the issue. He inspires a new vision of the 'joy of living' — convincing them they can feel better, not just live longer. That means enjoying the things that make daily life pleasurable, like making love or even taking long walks without the pain caused by their disease. 'Joy is a more powerful motivator than fear,' he says."

This exact approach makes a difference for my clients. And it can for you, too. Simply look for a positive motivator — and believe it's possible to achieve — and stuckness disappears.

Rather than focus on how alone you'll be when that cheating boyfriend is out of your life, think about how wonderful it will be to find a loyal and faithful partner. Rather than beat yourself up for not losing weight, think about all you will be able to do when you're healthier. Rather than dwell on how horrible it was to be fired, consider how great it will be to get a paycheck again.

Hey, if you're stuck in some area of your life, here's your homework: take out a piece of paper. Write one sentence about where you're stuck. Then write down what the happy outcome will be when you get unstuck. Shift it, baby. Then hold on to that positive glimmer and make a couple of teeny-tiny steps every day directly toward it.

It's not "change or die", my darlings, it's "change and be happy". And I'm here to tell you — it's completely possible.

Solving Problems

EVER FEEL LIKE THE WORLD IS CHOCK FULL OF PROBLEMS? There's a problem here, a problem there, and every problem screams for a solution. Ever consider how your life change if you knew, in your very marrow, that you are not responsible for fixing every problem in the world?

An emotional sponge takes on problems like a city bus takes on passengers — and ends up feeling overloaded. Plenty of these good folk become my clients because they just can't cope with their burdens.

You know the type. They're the resilient, strong person who has faced plenty of adversity and has developed a sense that there's nothing they can't solve. Their shoulders are broad, and they can carry a huge load. So they keep taking on one tangled situation after another. They carry their kid's problems, their co-worker's problems, their mother's problems, their neighbor's problems and the problems of the woman in front of them in the checkout line. Her biggest complaint? Never enough time.

The emotional sponge can also be the person who defines himself by a willingness to "help". They want to lend a hand, pitch in, offer support. As a result, they say yes to everything. They organize every charity drive, political leafletting effort and recycling program in a hundred mile radius. And they're frazzled.

One more type of emotional sponge — the person who's so uncertain about her own feelings so she takes on the emotions of those around her. If everyone else is worried about the price of tea in China, she adopts that worry as her own. Like a pinball, she bounces from feeling to feeling, and ends up drained and exhausted.

I was blessed to have a son who had no interest in tying his own shoes — especially if I was limitlessly willing to get down on my knees and tie them for him. One day I realized that if he didn't learn to tie his shoes himself I might have to visit his college campus daily (not in my plan for 2012, honestly). When I stopped solving his problem for him, he learned to tie his shoes.

And so it is. Maybe we solve other people's problems because it makes us feel useful, or needed, or — maybe we can admit this — slightly superior. Regardless, when you take on the problems of others you prevent them from learning the skills to prioritize and solve their own problems.

Your "help" may actually make the problem persist.

Becoming real — being comfortable in your own skin with who you are — absolutely requires coming to terms with the idea that you are not responsible for fixing every problem in the world.

In fact, not every problem can be solved. (Death is permanent, for instance.)

Not every problem should be solved. (Because time alone may resolve it.)

And not every problem is really a problem. (We just make it so to satisfy our own needs.)

If you plant a seed in dirt, and water it, you don't know whether it's growing until a sprout shoots up. If you're worried about its progress and dig up the seed, you'll kill the plant.

The best course of action is to wait. Leave it alone. And trust.

Which is exactly what you do when you step back from the responsibility for fixing every problem. Wait. Watch. Trust.

And, chances are, when you stop solving the problems of the world, you'll have the time you need to focus on the problems that really matter — your own.

෴

Pay For It

Knowing when to ask for help is a hallmark of health.

Not a sign of weakness.

Or of moral collapse.

Nope, asking for help is a sign of self-awareness and strength.

And I am feeling quite self-aware and strong right now because I not only asked for help, but I got it. I was so serious about getting help, darlings, that I paid for it.

When I'm willing to pay, I know I'm serious.

Now, for someone who has written a book with "De-clutter" in the title, you may find it odd to hear that I hired a de-clutterer. But I did. And it may just be the best money I've spent in a long time. Because what had been a problem area – an unfinished storage area in my basement stuffed to the rafters with junk – has changed from being a stinking, rotting albatross around my neck to a chirpy Bluebird of Happiness on my shoulder.

I've thrown away 15 boxes full of junk. Nine large green trash bags of... trash. I have sorted toys and clothes and a huge pile of stuff is going to Goodwill. And what I'm keeping is stuff I want, or is useful, or is loved.

I feel so relieved. And happy that the thing I no longer need might be just the thing someone else will love.

And I couldn't have done it on my own. I know this. How? Because I routinely went down there, trash bags in hand, opened the door, full of intention to Clean This Place Up, and got immediately overwhelmed. Where to start? How to start? I'd usually end up heaving a huge sigh as I turned on my heel, snapped off the light and shut the door. Until I got up the courage to go down there again, which would always end in the same frustrating and diminishing result: nothing done.

By getting the right kind of help this week, I was able to get the right kind of result.

So that's why I hired a coach, too.

For someone who is a coach, you may find it odd to hear that I hired a coach. But I did. And it just may be the best money I've spent in a long time. Because I was able to get clear on some very important things about my business and my life. Clear enough to make really good decisions.

Now, I have to say that I'm one lucky woman. I am in a circle of exceptional, generous coaches who coach each other on an as-needed basis. It's a tremendous gift and I am very grateful for the connection with these wonderful people. But there is something that happens when you pay for what you need. Maybe you take it more seriously, because you're invested. Maybe it has to do with making a commitment. Maybe the formality of sending a check amps the meaning up a bit.

Regardless. By working with a coach, I will be a better coach. A happier person. And that's a great "get".

So, let's talk about you. Where do you need help?

Can you identify the results you'd like? And find the perfect person to help you get there?

Can you call them today? And to prove that you're serious about getting this thing done, pay them?

Because, trust me, your life will be so much better when you do.

༄

Do Less, Get More

WE'VE ALWAYS BEEN TOLD THAT "TO MAKE SOUND decisions, people must consciously, deliberately, weigh their options", but, surprisingly, that strategy only works with the simplest problems. New research shows that the tougher the choice, the less you need to agonize over it. When faced with a tough situation, you need to go with your gut and be *less* conscious.

It's weird to think that big decisions need the least deliberation, isn't it? But, it's all about where you're putting your time and energy. You may know that I have the 100 Units of Energy Theory — you have 100 units of energy to spend each day. No more, no less. Can't use yesterday's because they're gone, and you can't borrow from tomorrow's because they belong to tomorrow.

You got 100. How you use them is up to you.

And here's how you do less and get more: if you're agonizing over a complex decision — using, say 75 units of energy a day on it... for weeks — then shift into unconscious thought and just make a choice. The research shows that you'll likely make an excellent decision, and you'll free up tons of energy to do other things.

Do (worry) less, get more done.

What about the office? How do you do less when there's so much to do?

This is going to sound counter-intuitive, I admit it. But to be more effective at work, you also need to be less conscious. In fact, what you need to do is care *less*.

The odd paradox is that when people have a crisis like an illness, or an outside interest like a fundraiser, sports tournament, or college search, their performance at work often *improves*. It's in these periods that we use our time wisely, meet our objectives and serve our priorities.

We allocate our energy units effectively.

And feel really good about our lives.

So, if you are swamped and feel like there is too much to do and not enough time… focus on your priorities, make good, unconscious decisions, and you will find that you are able to do less, and get much, much more.

༄

The Simplest Solution

Ever heard of Occam's Razor? William of Ockham was a 14th century monk who labored in Latin on matters of logic. His key observation, translated and traveled through the centuries, is called "Occam's Razor" (obviously spelling mutated over time):

"All other things being equal, the simplest solution is the best."

What's this mean for your life?

When you have a problem with someone else: what's the simplest solution? Would it be... telling Karen, who talks to Alex, who mentions something to Tom, who plays golf with the husband of the person you have a problem with? Will that approach solve your problem, or potentially make it worse? Using Occam's Razor to cut away the extraneous steps, we find the simplest solution — *talking with the person directly* to handle the problem.

How do you know when you're not using the simplest solution? When you find yourself saying, "I can't", as in "I can't find a new job at my age because I'd have to go back to school, and pass that exam, get certified, and probably move to some new city, which would be really hard on John and the kids." Rather complicated scenario, huh? It's a solution which — surprise, surprise — successfully keeps you from doing anything at all. Can we discover the simplest solution?

Could it be to find a great job that provides training right in your own home town?

Sometimes it seems we love having the problem so very much that we envision only completely unworkable, complicated solutions — just so we can hang on to the problem we say we hate (but actually love). It's like: "I need a job but don't want a job but want to revel in what a screw-up I am 'cuz I'm not getting a job." How can we love and hate a problem at the same time? It's called story fondling, and it reinforces negative stuff and keeps us totally and completely stuck in the past.

Identifying the simplest solution is a way to cut through all the debris in your life and find a really good, clean place to be. The simplest solution is always authentic. The simplest solution is easy. The simplest solution is the way to go.

So, when you find yourself tied up in knots trying to find a complicated solution to whatever you face, think of good old William of Ockham and ask yourself: "All other things being equal, what's the simplest solution?"

⁓

Start At The End

In the seminal, thought-provoking, deeply spiritual film, "The Sound Of Music", one of Rodgers and Hammerstein's songs goes:

Let's start at the very beginning

A very good place to start

When you read you begin with A-B-C

When you sing you begin with do-re-mi

Do-re-mi, do-re-mi

The first three notes just happen to be

Do-re-mi, do-re-mi

But, I'm going to turn that familiar refrain on its ear.

Because if you really want to change something in your life, *you have to start at the very end.*

You have to start with an idea of what it is you want, and allow yourself to understand what it will be like, what it will feel like, to have achieved the change you seek.

Perhaps you've heard of the *Seven Habits of Highly Effective People*. Stephen Covey wrote that little book — and it's sold a kajillion billion copies since it came out in 1989. OK, to be really honest, only two of his Habits made me sit up and say, "Yes!" It was "Seek first to understand, then be understood" that helped re-orient my communication style, and "start with the end in mind" which gave me a framework for planning.

You know, it seems as though so many of us are on the way somewhere. But if asked, we don't really know what the destination might be. We meander and lollygag and sniff corners, but, thank goodness, we don't get off track! Because there's absolutely no track to get off in the first place.

Because we're starting at the beginning and not focusing on the end.

Is there something you want to do in your life? Get promoted? Get married? Lose weight, find love, de-clutter, save money, perhaps? (Funny how my book title naturally works its way into so many places, isn't it?)

Whatever you want to do, start with the end in mind.

Tell me: What will it be like when you are the director of your office? When you lose 30 pounds? When you find true love? When you work for yourself? Inhabit those feelings. Visualize what your life will be like. Face any fears that come up and deal with them.

See, hear, feel, smell and taste what it will be like when you have what you want.

And by doing so you will be giving yourself a vision. A destination to point toward. You will have created a road map to your own success.

You will know what to do, and how to get there — because you know exactly where to go.

If you are meandering or stuck in the journey of your life, pull over into a quiet rest stop and ask yourself, "What do I want more than anything, right now?"

And with that end in mind, you can get started.

Acknowledgements

Writing is, by its very nature, a rather solitary pursuit. However, I am blessed with a virtual crowd without whom this book would not have come to fruition.

First, to my readers, who offer ideas, suggestions and insight into what I do. Thank you. Knowing that you read my stuff every week is the carrot at the end of the stick that keeps me going.

My friends on Facebook and Twitter who read my posts and send them around to all of their friends – you have helped me grow in so many ways. I thank you.

Friends like Pam Slim, Hiro Boga, Patti Digh, Jen Louden, Laurie Foley, Jennifer Voss, Lynne Gillis, Koren Motekaitis, Ann Mehl, Chris Brandt, Kay Ballard… you motivate me and inspire me to reach higher and dig deeper. Je t'adore.

Then there's Joe Munroe, Betsey Kirkemo, Sally Giedrys, Julie Petersmeyer, Shelby Scarbrough, Maralyn Marsteller, Jill Collins – one word from any of these kind people and I'm immediately back on the right track.

Most of all, this book was written with the spirit of my great friend and mentor, Anne Wexler, over my right shoulder, as ever. Because she was who she was, I am who I am.

Finally, to thank my valiant, understanding and eye-rolling teenaged children – Munroe and Grace Woodward – who give me space when I write, and suffer in silence when I try out a line or theme while driving them to school, or to practice, or to Madeline's or Tim's house. Without you, without your love and support, I would not be who I am today. And to you, I am profoundly and humbly grateful.

About the Author

MICHELE WOODWARD IS A CAREER STRATEGIST, MASTER Certified Coach, author, speaker and teacher, who helps people get clear about who they are and what they want to do – and develop a workable action plan to get where they want to go. She is the author of **Lose Weight, Find Love, De-Clutter & Save Money: Essays on Happier Living**, available at Amazon.com and is the founder of Career Invention Coach Training (www.careerinvention.com) – focused on training coaches to understand the new rules of work - and Kick Ass Mentoring (www.kickassmentoring.com) – a marketing training program for coaches. She's thrived in a number of high-level, high-pressure positions – at The White House, in corporate America – and has served as an advisor to entrepreneurs. Michele is a sought-after speaker, leads a number of workshops and classes, and writes a popular blog. She lives outside Washington, DC, with two teenagers, two puppies and an optimistic outlook.

Made in the USA
Lexington, KY
01 August 2010